2016 SQA Past Papers With Answers

National 5
ENGLISH

National 5 ENGLISH

SQA

2014, 2015 & 2016 Exams

HODDER
GIBSON
AN HACHETTE UK COMPANY

This book contains the official SQA 2014, 2015 and 2016 Exams for National 5 English, with associated SQA-approved answers modified from the official marking instructions that accompany the paper.

In addition the book contains study skills advice. This advice has been specially commissioned by Hodder Gibson, and has been written by experienced senior teachers and examiners in line with the new National 5 syllabus and assessment outlines. This is not SQA material but has been devised to provide further guidance for National 5 examinations.

Hodder Gibson is grateful to the copyright holders, as credited on the final page of the Answer section, for permission to use their material. Every effort has been made to trace the copyright holders and to obtain their permission for the use of copyright material. Hodder Gibson will be happy to receive information allowing us to rectify any error or omission in future editions.

Hachette UK's policy is to use papers that are natural, renewable and recyclable products and made from wood grown in sustainable forests. The logging and manufacturing processes are expected to conform to the environmental regulations of the country of origin.

Orders: please contact Bookpoint Ltd, 130 Park Drive, Milton Park, Abingdon, Oxon OX14 4SE. Telephone: (44) 01235 827720. Fax: (44) 01235 400454. Lines are open 9.00–5.00, Monday to Saturday, with a 24-hour message answering service. Visit our website at www.hoddereducation.co.uk. Hodder Gibson can be contacted direct on: Tel: 0141 333 4650; Fax: 0141 404 8188; email: hoddergibson@hodder.co.uk

This collection first published in 2016 by
Hodder Gibson, an imprint of Hodder Education,
An Hachette UK Company
211 St Vincent Street
Glasgow G2 5QY

Typeset by Aptara, Inc.

Printed in the UK

A catalogue record for this title is available from the British Library

ISBN: 978-1-4718-9108-3

3 2 1

2017 2016

Introduction

Study Skills – what you need to know to pass exams!

Pause for thought

Many students might skip quickly through a page like this. After all, we all know how to revise. Do you really though?

Think about this:

"IF YOU ALWAYS DO WHAT YOU ALWAYS DO, YOU WILL ALWAYS GET WHAT YOU HAVE ALWAYS GOT."

Do you like the grades you get? Do you want to do better? If you get full marks in your assessment, then that's great! Change nothing! This section is just to help you get that little bit better than you already are.

There are two main parts to the advice on offer here. The first part highlights fairly obvious things but which are also very important. The second part makes suggestions about revision that you might not have thought about but which WILL help you.

Part 1

DOH! It's so obvious but …

Start revising in good time

Don't leave it until the last minute – this will make you panic.

Make a revision timetable that sets out work time AND play time.

Sleep and eat!

Obvious really, and very helpful. Avoid arguments or stressful things too – even games that wind you up. You need to be fit, awake and focused!

Know your place!

Make sure you know exactly **WHEN and WHERE** your exams are.

Know your enemy!

Make sure you know what to expect in the exam.

How is the paper structured?

How much time is there for each question?

What types of question are involved?

Which topics seem to come up time and time again?

Which topics are your strongest and which are your weakest?

Are all topics compulsory or are there choices?

Learn by DOING!

There is no substitute for past papers and practice papers – they are simply essential! Tackling this collection of papers and answers is exactly the right thing to be doing as your exams approach.

Part 2

People learn in different ways. Some like low light, some bright. Some like early morning, some like evening / night. Some prefer warm, some prefer cold. But everyone uses their BRAIN and the brain works when it is active. Passive learning – sitting gazing at notes – is the most INEFFICIENT way to learn anything. Below you will find tips and ideas for making your revision more effective and maybe even more enjoyable. What follows gets your brain active, and active learning works!

Activity 1 – Stop and review

Step 1

When you have done no more than 5 minutes of revision reading STOP!

Step 2

Write a heading in your own words which sums up the topic you have been revising.

Step 3

Write a summary of what you have revised in no more than two sentences. Don't fool yourself by saying, "I know it, but I cannot put it into words". That just means you don't know it well enough. If you cannot write your summary, revise that section again, knowing that you must write a summary at the end of it. Many of you will have notebooks full of blue/black ink writing. Many of the pages will not be especially attractive or memorable so try to liven them up a bit with colour as you are reviewing and rewriting. **This is a great memory aid, and memory is the most important thing.**

Activity 2 — Use technology!

Why should everything be written down? Have you thought about "mental" maps, diagrams, cartoons and colour to help you learn? And rather than write down notes, why not record your revision material?

What about having a text message revision session with friends? Keep in touch with them to find out how and what they are revising and share ideas and questions.

Why not make a video diary where you tell the camera what you are doing, what you think you have learned and what you still have to do? No one has to see or hear it, but the process of having to organise your thoughts in a formal way to explain something is a very important learning practice.

Be sure to make use of electronic files. You could begin to summarise your class notes. Your typing might be slow, but it will get faster and the typed notes will be easier to read than the scribbles in your class notes. Try to add different fonts and colours to make your work stand out. You can easily Google relevant pictures, cartoons and diagrams which you can copy and paste to make your work more attractive and **MEMORABLE**.

Activity 3 – This is it. Do this and you will know lots!

Step 1

In this task you must be very honest with yourself! Find the SQA syllabus for your subject (www.sqa.org.uk). Look at how it is broken down into main topics called MANDATORY knowledge. That means stuff you MUST know.

Step 2

BEFORE you do ANY revision on this topic, write a list of everything that you already know about the subject. It might be quite a long list but you only need to write it once. It shows you all the information that is already in your long-term memory so you know what parts you do not need to revise!

Step 3

Pick a chapter or section from your book or revision notes. Choose a fairly large section or a whole chapter to get the most out of this activity.

With a buddy, use Skype, Facetime, Twitter or any other communication you have, to play the game "If this is the answer, what is the question?". For example, if you are revising Geography and the answer you provide is "meander", your buddy would have to make up a question like "What is the word that describes a feature of a river where it flows slowly and bends often from side to side?".

Make up 10 "answers" based on the content of the chapter or section you are using. Give this to your buddy to solve while you solve theirs.

Step 4

Construct a wordsearch of at least 10 X 10 squares. You can make it as big as you like but keep it realistic. Work together with a group of friends. Many apps allow you to make wordsearch puzzles online. The words and phrases can go in any direction and phrases can be split. Your puzzle must only contain facts linked to the topic you are revising. Your task is to find 10 bits of information to hide in your puzzle, but you must not repeat information that you used in Step 3. DO NOT show where the words are. Fill up empty squares with random letters. Remember to keep a note of where your answers are hidden but do not show your friends. When you have a complete puzzle, exchange it with a friend to solve each other's puzzle.

Step 5

Now make up 10 questions (not "answers" this time) based on the same chapter used in the previous two tasks. Again, you must find NEW information that you have not yet used. Now it's getting hard to find that new information! Again, give your questions to a friend to answer.

Step 6

As you have been doing the puzzles, your brain has been actively searching for new information. Now write a NEW LIST that contains only the new information you have discovered when doing the puzzles. Your new list is the one to look at repeatedly for short bursts over the next few days. Try to remember more and more of it without looking at it. After a few days, you should be able to add words from your second list to your first list as you increase the information in your long-term memory.

FINALLY! Be inspired...

Make a list of different revision ideas and beside each one write **THINGS I HAVE** tried, **THINGS I WILL** try and **THINGS I MIGHT** try. Don't be scared of trying something new.

And remember – "FAIL TO PREPARE AND PREPARE TO FAIL!"

National 5 English

The course

The National 5 English course aims to enable you to develop the ability to:

- Listen, talk, read and write, as appropriate to purpose, audience and context
- Understand, analyse and evaluate texts, including Scottish texts, as appropriate to purpose and audience in the contexts of literature, language and media
- Create and produce texts, as appropriate to purpose, audience and context
- Apply knowledge and understanding of language.

How the course is graded

The grade you finally get for National 5 English depends on three things:

- The two internal Unit Assessments you do in school or college: "Analysis and Evaluation" and "Creation and Production"; these don't count towards the final grade, but you must have passed them before you can get a final grade
- Your Portfolio of Writing – this is submitted in April for marking by SQA and counts for 30% of your final grade
- The two exams you sit in May – that's what this book is all about.

The exams

Reading for Understanding, Analysis and Evaluation

- Exam time: 1 hour
- Total marks: 30
- Weighting in final grade: 30%
- What you have to do: read a passage and answer questions about it.

Critical Reading

- Exam time: 1 hour 30 minutes
- Total marks: 40 (20 for each section)
- Weighting in final grade: 40%
- What you have to do: Section 1: read an extract from one of the Scottish Texts which are set for National 5 and answer questions about it; Section 2: write an essay about a work of literature you have studied during your course.

Reading for Understanding, Analysis and Evaluation

Three important tips to start with

- Since there will usually be a question asking you to summarise some or all of the passage, it is really important to read the whole passage before you even look at the questions. Doing this will give you a chance to get a rough idea of the main ideas in the passage, and you can add to this as you work your way through the questions.
- Pay close attention to the number of marks available for each question and make sure your answer is appropriate to the number of marks. In most questions, you will get 1 mark for each correct point.
- Some questions tell you to "use your own words". This means you mustn't just copy chunks from the passage – you have to show that you understand what it means by rephrasing it in your own words.

Questions which ask for understanding

- Keep your answers fairly short and pay attention to the number of marks available.

Questions about language features

- This type of question will ask you to comment on features such as Word Choice, Imagery, Sentence Structure and Tone.
- You should pick out a relevant language feature and make a valid comment about its impact. Try to make your comments as specific as possible and avoid vague comments (like "It is a good word to use because it gives me a clear picture of what the writer is saying"). Some hints:

  - **Word Choice:** always try to pick a single word or expression and then give its connotations, i.e. what it **suggests**

  - **Sentence Structure:** don't just name the feature – try to explain what effect it achieves **in that particular sentence**

  - **Imagery:** try to explain what the image means **literally** and then go on to explain what the writer is **suggesting** by using that image

- **Tone**   this is always difficult – a good tip is to imagine the sentence or paragraph being read out loud and try to spot how the words or the structure give it a particular tone.

Summary questions

- Make sure you follow the instruction about what it is you are to summarise (the question will be as helpful as possible).
- Stick to the main ideas; avoid unimportant points and never include examples.
- Make sure you earn all the marks available for the question.

Critical Reading

Section 1 – Scottish Text

The most important thing to remember here is that there are two very different types of question to be answered:

- Three or four questions (for a total of 12 marks) which focus entirely on the extract
- One question (for 8 marks) which requires knowledge of the whole text (or of another poem or short story by the same writer).

The first type of question will often ask you to use the same type of close textual analysis skills you used in the Reading part of your Analysis and Evaluation Unit. There can also be a question asking for the type of summary skills you're used to in the Reading part of the exam. The golden rule is to read each question very carefully and do exactly as instructed.

The last question for 8 marks can be answered **either** in bullet points **or** as a "mini essay". Choose whichever approach you are more comfortable with. Make as many relevant points as you can. If you look at the Marking Guide which is used for this type of question (see page 116), you'll get an idea of how this question is marked and this should help you in your approach.

Final bit of advice for the Scottish Text question: when you see the extract in the exam paper, don't get too confident just because you recognise it (you certainly should recognise it if you've studied properly!) And even if you've answered questions on it before, remember that the questions in the exam are likely to be different, so stay alert.

Section 2 – Critical Essay

A common mistake is to rely too heavily on ideas and whole paragraphs you have used in practice essays and try to use them for the question you have chosen in the exam. The trick is to come to the exam with lots of ideas and thoughts about at least one of the texts you have studied and use these to tackle the question you choose from the exam paper. You mustn't use the exam question as an excuse to trot out an answer you've prepared in advance.

Structure

Every good essay has a structure, but there is no "correct" structure, no magic formula that the examiners are looking for. It's **your** essay, so structure it the way **you** want. As long as you're answering the question all the way through, then you'll be fine.

Relevance

Be relevant to the question **all the time** – not just in the first and last paragraphs.

Central concerns

Try to make sure your essay shows that you have thought about and understood the central concerns of the text, i.e. what it's "about" – the ideas and themes the writer is exploring in the text.

Quotations

In poetry and drama essays, you're expected to quote from the text, but never fall into the trap of learning a handful of quotations and forcing them all into the essay regardless of the question you're answering. In prose essays, quotation is much less important, and you can show your knowledge much more effectively by referring in detail to what happens in key sections of the novel or the short story.

Techniques

You are expected to show some understanding of how various literary techniques work within a text, but simply naming them will not get you marks, and structuring your essay around techniques rather than around relevant ideas in the text is not a good idea.

Good luck!

Remember that the rewards for passing National 5 English are well worth it! Your pass will help you get the future you want for yourself. In the exam, be confident in your own ability. If you're not sure how to answer a question, trust your instincts and just give it a go anyway – keep calm and don't panic! GOOD LUCK!

NATIONAL 5

2014

 National Qualifications 2014

X724/75/01

English
Reading for Understanding,
Analysis and Evaluation

WEDNESDAY, 30 APRIL
1:00 PM – 2:00 PM

Total marks — 30

Attempt ALL questions.

Write your answers clearly in the answer booklet provided. In the answer booklet you must clearly identify the question number you are attempting.

Use **blue** or **black** ink.

Before leaving the examination room you must give your answer booklet to the Invigilator; if you do not you may lose all the marks for this paper.

Hey, parents, leave those kids alone.

In many ways, nothing changes. We love our children. We want our children to grow up to be competent, decent human beings fit for adult purpose. These are the main things, and in these we have, I think we are all agreed, not done too badly. Our children, and I'll generalise here, are not serial axe murderers or kitten drowners. Our children do make an
5 effort — at least on special occasions anyway — to repay the enormous investment of time, energy, money and emotion we have poured into them. Children are programmed to please, to be loved, and to love us back.

So we are not here to examine our children. What we should do is try to find out where we have gone so terribly wrong. Before we come to the wretchedly indulgent state of
10 modern parenting, though, I suppose I'd better set out my stall. Inevitably, when one becomes a parent, one can't help revisiting one's own childhood to make comparisons.

When I was little, we were given no choices — about what we ate, what we wore, what we did, where we went to school, when we went to bed etc. I could only choose what to read.

15 There was not so much stuff (many of my son's 15-year-old friends have iPods, iPads, MacBooks, unlimited access to their parents' credit cards, Pay Pal, eBay and iTunes accounts — and not just iPhones, but BlackBerrys too), so we made our own fun.

Our parents provided us with the essentials, then got on with their own lives. Which makes me realise that my parents were brilliant, not for what they did, but more for
20 what they didn't do.

So we were fed, we were clothed, we were loved, and we had all the books we could read. But there was not the expectation of having every wish granted, as there is now, and that is the best thing that my parents could ever have given us.

I remember only once going to a restaurant in the UK. It was a motorway café on the
25 A303. My father told us, wincing as he looked at the laminated text, with its stomach-churning pictograms, that we could have the spag bol. From the children's menu.

We had a TV, but as we lived in Belgium there was nothing to watch apart from two American sitcoms, which came on only once a week.

My parents were so hard up that when we went to England for holidays on the family farm
30 on Exmoor — mainly spent "wooding" for winter fuel on rainswept hillsides — my father would invariably book cheap overnight ferry crossings from the Continent. He would never shell out for a cabin, despite the 1am or 3am departure slots. Instead, he would tell us to go to sleep in the back of the car, parked in the lower deck, where we would eventually pass out from suffocation or diesel fumes.

35 We never had friends round for "playdates". Keeping children busy and happy was not a parental priority. If we were bored, that was our own fault. In fact, there was nothing to do for weeks on end except rake leaves (my father once made us spend a whole half-term raking leaves) and read on our beds. Occasionally my mother would shout up the stairs: "Stop reading!" Imagine that now, when children are on their laptops in their rooms,
40 looking at . . . I don't even want to imagine.

As for school, well, reports were read, not dwelt upon, as they were not parents' business, but ours. As for parental involvement, all I can tell you is that my father's proudest boast as a parent is that he never, once, attended a parent-teacher meeting at any one of our schools.

45 It never did me any harm, but still, I can't repeat this sensible, caring regime of character-building, toughening, benign neglect for my own children . . . and nor, it appears, can anyone else. Now examples of "wet parenting" abound.

We also live in a world where a manic mum calls herself a Tiger Mother and writes a bestselling book by the same name about how to produce straight-A violin-playing tennis-champ superkids, and where pushy, anxious helicopter parents hover over every school. A friend reports that when her son was due to visit the Brecon Beacons on a school camping trip this summer, three mothers pulled out their sons because the weather forecast was "rainy".

University dons are also complaining of a traumatic level of parental over-involvement just at the exact moment that mummies and daddies are supposed to be letting go.

It was the complete opposite in my day. When I was on my gap year, I called my father from Israel in September and told him I'd decided not to take up my place at university. I announced that I wanted to stay in Galilee with a handsome local shepherd. For ever.

My father didn't miss a beat. "Great scheme!" he cried, astutely divining that if he approved the plan, I would never carry it out.

In my lifetime, parenthood has undergone a terrifying transition. Becoming a mother or father is no longer something you just are. It is something you do, like becoming a vet—complete with training courses, parenting vouchers, government targets and guidelines, and a host of academics and caring professionals (as well as their websites, and telephone helplines) on hand 24/7 to guide you through what to expect when your twentysomethings return home.

Parenting has become subsidised and professionalised, even though anyone can (and, frankly, does) have a baby, after which they become parents.

I love being a parent, most of the time anyway, but we should immediately de-professionalise it, on the grounds that: one, it's unpaid; and two, thanks to the economy, lack of housing and jobs etc, you never get to retire.

Rachel Johnson, in The Times

MARKS

1. Look at line 9, where the writer gives the view that, nowadays, parents "have gone . . . terribly wrong".

    Explain **in your own words** what the writer goes on to say has gone wrong.   2

2. Explain any way in which the sentences in lines 12 – 14 help to provide a link between ideas at this point in the passage.   2

3. Look at lines 24 – 40, where the writer develops the idea of her family being "hard up".

    Show fully how examples of the writer's use of such features of language as **word choice** or **sentence structure** helps to convey her ideas effectively.   4

4. Look at lines 45 – 47.

    Explain what is meant by the expression "benign neglect", and explain what is surprising about this expression.   3

5. Look at lines 48 – 55.

    With reference to **three** examples of the writer's **word choice** from these lines, show fully how she makes clear her disapproval of what she calls "wet parenting".   6

6. In the expression "straight-A violin-playing tennis-champ superkids" the writer tries to achieve a humorous, mocking tone.

    Explain with reference to her use of language how successful you think she has been in achieving this tone.   2

7. Look at lines 59 – 60.

    Show fully how the writer conveys her father's **apparent** attitude, and his **actual attitude**, to her plan.   4

8. Look at lines 61 – 66, and then explain **as far as possible in your own words** what similarities the writer sees between "Becoming a mother or father" and "becoming a vet".   2

9. In this article, the writer points out several differences between parenting and childhood when she was little and parenting and childhood now (she refers to "a terrifying transition", line 61).

    As far as possible in your own words, summarise what some main differences are.   5

[END OF QUESTION PAPER]

National Qualifications 2014

X724/75/02

English
Critical Reading

WEDNESDAY, 30 APRIL

2:20 PM – 3:50 PM

Total marks — 40

SECTION 1 — Scottish Text — 20 marks

Read an extract from a Scottish text you have previously studied.

Choose ONE text from either

Part A — Drama	Pages 2–7
or	
Part B — Prose	Pages 8–17
or	
Part C — Poetry	Pages 18–25

Attempt ALL the questions for your chosen text.

SECTION 2 — Critical Essay — 20 marks

Attempt ONE question from the following genres — Drama, Prose, Poetry, Film and Television Drama, or Language.

Your answer must be on a different genre from that chosen in Section 1.

You should spend approximately 45 minutes on each Section.

Write your answers clearly in the answer booklet provided. In the answer booklet you must clearly identify the question number you are attempting.

Use **blue** or **black** ink.

Before leaving the examination room you must give your answer booklet to the Invigilator; if you do not you may lose all the marks for this paper.

SECTION 1 — SCOTTISH TEXT — 20 marks

PART A — SCOTTISH TEXT — DRAMA

Text 1 — Drama

If you choose this text you may not attempt a question on Drama in Section 2.

Read the extract below and then attempt the following questions.

Bold Girls by Rona Munro

Marie's house. Belfast. Late afternoon. Present day

It is irons and ironing boards and piles of clothes waiting to be smoothed, socks and pegs and damp sheets waiting for a break in the Belfast drizzle for the line; it's toys in pieces and toys that are just cardboard boxes and toys that are new and gleaming and flashing
5 *with lights and have swallowed up the year's savings. It's pots and pans and steam and the kettle always hot for tea; it's furniture that's bald with age and a hearth in front of the coal fire that's gleaming clean.*

At the moment it's empty, an unnatural, expectant emptiness that suggests this room is never deserted; it's too stuffed with human bits and pieces, all the clutter of housework
10 *and life.*

There is a small picture of the virgin on one wall, a large grainy blow-up photo of a smiling young man on the other. He has a seventies haircut and moustache.

Deirdre is not in this room, she is crouching on all fours on her own talking out of darkness in which only her face is visible. She is wary, young.

15 DEIRDRE: (*moving from all fours*) The sun is going down behind the hills, the sky is grey. There's hills at the back there, green. I can't hardly see them because the stones between here and there are grey, the street is grey. Somewhere a bird is singing and falling in the sky. I hear the ice cream van and the traffic and the helicopter overhead.

Black-out; after a few minutes Lights come up on Marie's house.

20 *Marie bursts into the room with her arms laden with four packets of crisps, two of Silk Cut and a packet of chocolate biscuits. She is cheerful, efficient, young. She drops one of the crisps, tuts in exasperation, and looks at it*

MARIE: (*shouting back out the door*) Mickey! Mickey were you wanting smoky bacon?... Well this is salt and vinegar . . . Well, why did you not say? Away you and swap this . . .
25 Catch now. (*She hurls the bag*) No you cannot . . . No . . . because you'll not eat your tea if you do! (*At the doorway*) Mickey, pick up those crisps and don't be so bold.

Marie comes back into the room and starts two jobs simultaneously. First she puts the crisps etc away, then she fills a pan with water and throws it on the stove. She starts sorting her dry washing into what needs ironing and what doesn't; she sorts a few items
30 *then starts peeling potatoes; all her movements have a frenetic efficiency.*

MARKS

Questions

1. Look at the description of Marie's house. By referring to word choice and/or sentence structure, explain what impression this creates of Marie's daily life.

   4

2. With close reference to the text, explain what Deirdre's **actions** and **speech** tell us about her relationship to her surroundings. You could consider: word choice, tone, the use of imagery etc . . .

   4

3. The playwright introduces Marie. What do we find out about:

   (a) her attitude towards Mickey;

   2

   (b) her attitude towards her daily routine?

   2

4. The play goes on to develop our understanding of how challenging life is in many respects for the "bold girls". By referring to this extract and at least one other example from the play, discuss what these challenges are.

   8

[Turn over

OR

Text 2 — Drama

If you choose this text you may not attempt a question on Drama in Section 2.

Read the extract below and then attempt the following questions.

Sailmaker by Alan Spence

Extract from Act Two

ALEC:		Look at the state ae us. We're livin like bloody Steptoe and Son! Nae light. Place is like a midden. When did we last gie it a good clean? Needs gutted.
		Look at it!
DAVIE:		It's hard son. It's no easy on yer own.
5	ALEC:	So ye go an get bevvied. Forget it all.
	DAVIE:	Ye'd think ah came in steamin every night!
		Christ ah need a wee break once in a while. Like the night. Nae harm in it. Good company. Wee sing song. Right gents, a wee bit order there. One singer one song. That lassie's a rare singer. Sang Honky Tonk Angels.
10		She's the one ah told ye about.
	ALEC:	(*Sarcastic*) The really nice person.
	DAVIE:	She wis.
	ALEC:	Who was that lady I saw you with last night?
	DAVIE:	That was no lady, that was a really nice person.
15		Nae harm in it.
	ALEC:	It's always the same. Every time ye meet a wumman she's a really really really nice person.
		Why don't ye just admit that ye fancy her?
		(DAVIE *slaps him, exits*)
20		Ach aye, yirra good boy son. Wallop!
		Bad. Bad. Bad.
		(*Pause*)
		Wallop.
		(*Darkness. Spotlight on* ALEC)
25		I keep goin back.
		What is it I'm tryin to remember?
		What is it I'm tryin to say?
		There's somethin I've lost. Something I've forgotten.
		Sometimes in the middle of the night . . .
30		What is it I'm looking for?
		God knows.

MARKS

Questions

5. **In your own words**, summarise what happens in this part of the play. Make **two** key points.

2

6. Think about how Alec and Davie are feeling during their dialogue with one another (lines 1—19).

   (a) Show how Alec's language reflects his feelings.

2

   (b) Although he does not say very much, Davie experiences a range of emotions during his dialogue with his son. With close reference to the text, explain what **at least two** of these are.

4

7. Alec is left alone at the end of this extract.

   With reference to word-choice and sentence structure, explain clearly his state of mind at this stage in the play.

4

8. By referring to this extract, and to elsewhere in the play, explain how the character of Alec develops and changes as he grows older.

8

[Turn over

OR

Text 3 — Drama

If you choose this text you may not attempt a question on Drama in Section 2.

Read the extract below and then attempt the following questions.

Tally's Blood **by Ann Marie di Mambro**

This scene takes place in the back of the Pedreschi's shop.

ROSINELLA: You see the way Italians are getting on now, eh? Beginning to make a wee bit money? Because they're prepared to WORK that's why. I don't know anybody who works so hard as the Italian men.

Hughie in: with pail and mop.

5   HUGHIE: That's the tables cleared and the front shop mopped, Mrs Pedreschi, and the chip pan cleaned out. Is the milk boiled?

ROSINELLA: Should be.

She turns attention back to Lucia, Hughie lifts pot from stove and pours contents into two pails: he covers them and sets them aside, working like a trojan.

10   ROSINELLA: And the way they love their families. Nobody loves their families like the Italians. You want to stay for a wee bit pasta, Hughie? It's your favourite. Rigatoni.

HUGHIE: No thanks, Mrs Pedreschi. I better get up the road. Bridget's going out and I don't like my mammy left on her own.

15   ROSINELLA: Bridget's going out is she? Don't tell me she's winching?

HUGHIE: No. Her and Davie are going up to Charmaine's the night — to go over all the arrangements. My mammy's no up to it.

ROSINELLA: That's right. When's the wedding now?

Hughie and Lucia exchange glances: he makes gesture of "go ahead" to her. Lucia shakes
20   *head.*

Hughie: Saturday.

ROSINELLA: And where are they going to stay?

HUGHIE: At Charmaine's.

ROSINELLA: It's funny that, isn't it, but that's the way they do it here. In Italy a girl
25   must go to her husband's house. That's why you must have land if you've got sons.

Massimo in.

ROSINELLA: So that'll be your mammy left with her eldest and her youngest, eh? I don't see your Bridget ever marrying, do you? You see, Lucia, there's a lot of
30   women Bridget's age no married. The war killed that many young men. I'm right there, amn't I Massimo?

MASSIMO: You got those pails ready, son?

HUGHIE: I'll bring them through.

MARKS

MASSIMO: And give's a hand to put these shutters up before you go.

35 *Hughie and Massimo out: Rosinella watches him go.*

ROSINELLA: I'm right about that Davie, amn't I Lucia? Give it five or six months, Hughie'll be telling us he's an uncle again. Mind you, I suppose his mother must feel it, right enough. Can you find me a wee envelope hen, a wee poke or something? What was I saying . . . ah yes . . . See what I mean
40 about Italian men. Just take that brother of Hughie's. Getting married on Saturday, give him two or three days and he'll be out DRINKING with his pals.

Rosinella shooshes up when Hughie comes in, followed by Massimo: all locked up. Massimo takes off his apron, reaches for a bottle of wine.

45 MASSIMO: Thanks, Hughie son. You want a wee glass of wine?

HUGHIE: I better not, Mr Pedreschi. I better get up the road.

ROSINELLA: Hang on a minute, son. (She has slipped a couple of notes into the poke, gives it to Hughie) Here, give this to your brother from me. Instead of a present. Help them out a wee bit, eh? (Hughie hangs back, embarrassed)
50 . . . Take it.

Questions

9. (*a*) Rosinella makes stereotypical statements about Italians and/or Scots which are shown to be false in this extract. Identify **two** statements and explain how the playwright shows they are false.   4

   (*b*) Explain how you think the audience would react to this falseness.   2

10. Think about the character Rosinella.

   (*a*) How is Rosinella shown to be kind or caring in this extract?   2

   (*b*) How is Rosinella shown to be unkind or unpleasant in this extract?   2

11. Identify **two** examples of colloquial or conversational language from the extract.   2

12. This extract deals with racial stereotypes. With close reference to this extract and elsewhere in the play explain how the issue of racism is explored.   8

[Turn over

PART B — SCOTTISH TEXT — PROSE

Text 1 — Prose

If you choose this text you may not attempt a question on Prose in Section 2.

Read the extract below and then attempt the following questions.

The Cone-Gatherers by Robin Jenkins.

In this extract, a deer hunt, at which Neil and Calum have been told to help out, is coming to its violent end.

The drive was nearly over. Only a hundred or so yards away were the waiting guns. Frightened by the noises approaching them from the rear, and apprehensive of the human silence ahead, the five roe deer were halted, their heads high in nervous alertness. When Calum saw them, his cry was of delight and friendship, and then of terrified warning as
5 the dogs too, and Duror, caught sight of them and rushed in pursuit. Silently, with marvellous grace and agility over such rough ground, the deer flew for the doom ahead. Their white behinds were like moving glints of sunlight; without them their tawny hides might not have been seen in the autumnal wood.

Calum no longer was one of the beaters; he too was a deer hunted by remorseless men.
10 Moaning and gasping, he fled after them, with no hope of saving them from slaughter but with the impulse to share it with them. He could not, however, be so swift or sure of foot. He fell and rose again; he avoided one tree only to collide with another close to it; and all the time he felt, as the deer must have, the indifference of all nature; of the trees, of tall withered stalks of willow herb, of the patches of blue sky, of bushes, of piles of cut
15 scrubwood, of birds lurking in branches, and of the sunlight: presences which might have been expected to help or at least sympathise.

The dogs barked fiercely. Duror fired his gun in warning to those waiting in the ride. Neil, seeing his brother rush into danger, roared to him to come back. All the beaters, except Charlie far in the rear, joined in the commotion; the wood resounded with their exultant
20 shouts. Realising this must be the finish or kill, Graham, recuperating on the road, hopped back over the fence into the wood and bellowed loudest of all.

As Duror bawled to his dogs to stop lest they interfered with the shooting, and as the deer hesitated before making the dash across the ride, Calum was quite close to them as silent, desperate, and heroic, they sprang forward to die or escape. When the guns
25 banged he did not, as Neil had vehemently warned him to do, fall flat on the ground and put his fingers in his ears. Instead, with wails of lament, he dashed on at demented speed and shot out onto the broad green ride to hear a deer screaming and see it, wounded in the breast and forelegs, scrabbling about on its hindquarters. Captain Forgan was feverishly reloading his guns to fire again. Calum saw no one else, not even the lady or Mr
30 Tulloch, who was standing by himself about twenty yards away.

Screaming in sympathy, heedless of the danger of being shot, Calum flung himself upon the deer, clasped it around the neck and tried to comfort it. Terrified more than ever, it dragged him about with it in its mortal agony. Its blood came off onto his face and hands.

While Captain Forgan, Young Roderick, and Lady Runcie-Campbell stood petrified by this
35 sight, Duror followed by his dogs came leaping out of the wood. He seemed to be laughing in some kind of berserk joy.

Questions

13. Look at the first paragraph and describe the changing emotions Calum experiences when he sees the deer.   **2**

14. In lines 5—8 how does the writer emphasise the sadness of what is about to happen to the deer?   **2**

15. Identify two examples of how the writer's language in lines 9—16 convey Calum's clumsy panic as he tries to help the hunted animals.   **2**

16. Look again at lines 24—33. Show how the writer conveys the chaos of the moment when Calum reaches and tries to help the wounded deer.   **4**

17. How unusual do you find Duror's reaction in lines 34—36 to Calum ruining the deer drive?   **2**

18. Discuss how Duror is portrayed in this extract and elsewhere in the novel.   **8**

[Turn over

OR

Text 2 — Prose

If you choose this text you may not attempt a question on Prose in Section 2.

Read the extract below and then attempt the following questions.

The Testament of Gideon Mack by James Robertson

I went running every second or third day. I ran not as a member of a club, not in training for competitions (although I have run marathons for charity), not even to keep fit (although it had that effect), but because I enjoyed it. Yes, running filled me with joy, contentment, as nothing else did. It took me out of myself. Also, it was how I released
5 the energy inside me: as if the fire blazing away in there was my fuel. If I went four days without a run, I grew hot and tense and felt as if my chest was about to explode. I *needed* to run. It was how I got the heat out of my system.

Running made me aware both of the countryside in which I lived and of my physical self. When I set off through the streets of Monimaskit, I could feel the disapproval of some of
10 my parishioners boring into the back of my neck — there was something just *no richt* about a minister in shorts, and sweating. But once out of the town I left all that behind me. I avoided traffic-heavy main roads and ran on narrow, deserted unclassifieds, farm tracks, paths that led me through woods and alongside fields and over burns. I ran along the shore, I ran up into the low hills, I ran beside the crashing of the sea on sand and
15 shingle and I ran above the roaring of the Keldo Water as it fought through the Black Jaws on its way to that sea. I loved the idea of myself — was this vanity? — running among the shadows of trees, against the backdrop of hills, in the echo of birdsong and bellowing cows. I could run for a couple of hours at a time if I chose, barely pausing at gates or stiles, sensitive to the different noises my trainers made when I went up or down a hill, or
20 when I moved from hard road to soft path or grass. Usually I ran in the late afternoon, the dead time between daytime appointments and evening visits and meetings, and I seldom met anybody else. A woman walking her dog, perhaps, or a couple of lads on their bikes. Sometimes the woman would recognise me and say hello. Sometimes she'd recognise me but pretend not to, embarrassed by the ministerial knees. If the boys had a clue who I
25 was, they never let on.

I loved that time of day in all seasons and all weathers, the bright hot stillness of summer and the dark moody dampness of winter. I loved it for itself, but running made it more special still. Running emptied my head of work, the Kirk, the world. Difficult issues and awkward individuals were repelled by the force of my energy, and their ghosts faded into
30 the trees. In Israel young fanatics with explosives strapped to their bodies were wiping themselves and busloads of hated strangers off the planet; insect species were being extinguished every five minutes in the Amazon forest; military coups were being bloodily launched in Africa; dams were being built in China, making tens of thousands homeless; but in Keldo Woods, alone and immune and having slipped his clerical collar, Gideon Mack
35 was running. Sometimes a line from a song or a hymn got trapped in my head and I ran to its rhythm, half-enjoying it and half-annoyed by it. Phrases from the Scriptures that became strange and mantra-like in the repetition: *Nec tamen consumebatur*; "The Lord is with thee, thou mighty man of valour"; MENE, MENE, TEKEL UPHARSIN. Sometimes I heard my own voice in there, bits of poems I'd read, things I wished I'd said at the right
40 moment, heroic and true things I might say in the future — nothing, as it's turned out, remotely connected with what I would actually say.

Sometimes I saw myself as I do now — as if in a film, splashing through puddles to a soundtrack by Vangelis: *when I run I feel God's pleasure*. But that was somebody else: Eric Liddell, the Flying Scotsman, a missionary, a kind of saint. *The loneliness of the*
45 *long-distance runner*: phrases like that would enter my head and bounce around in there as I ran; but that was someone else again, a Borstal boy, a figure of fiction. I was somewhere in between — an escapee from my professional hypocrisy, a minister off the leash, a creature neither wholly real nor wholly imagined, hurrying through an ancient landscape. Yes, even then I suspected what I now know to be true: that life itself is not
50 wholly real. Existence is one thing, life quite another: it is the ghost that haunts existence, the spirit that animates it. Running, whether in the rain or sun, felt like life.

Questions

19. Using examples from this extract to support your points, explain the different reasons why Gideon Mack enjoys running.   4

20. What does this extract reveal about Mack's attitude to his job? Give evidence from the extract to support your answer.   2

21. Look closely at the **language** used in this extract.

    (a) Show how **sentence structure** helps the reader understand how much Gideon Mack enjoys running.   3

    (b) Choose one example of **imagery** used to help the reader understand the importance of running to Gideon Mack and explain how it does so.   3

22. Discuss one aspect of Gideon Mack's character which features in this extract and is developed elsewhere in the novel.   8

[Turn over

OR

Text 3 — Prose

If you choose this text you may not attempt a question on Prose in Section 2.

Read the extract below and then attempt the following questions.

***Kidnapped* by Robert Louis Stevenson**

In this extract, which is from Chapter 9 of the novel, David Balfour sees Alan Breck Stewart for the first time as he arrives on the Covenant.

We had run down a boat in the fog, and she had parted in the midst and gone to the bottom with all her crew, but one. This man (as I heard afterwards) had been sitting in the stern as a passenger, while the rest were on the benches rowing. At the moment of the blow, the stern had been thrown into the air, and the man (having his hands free, and

5 for all he was encumbered with a frieze overcoat that came below his knees) had leaped up and caught hold of the brig's bowsprit. It showed he had luck and much agility and unusual strength, that he should have thus saved himself from such a pass. And yet, when the captain brought him into the round-house, and I set eyes on him for the first time, he looked as cool as I did.

10 He was smallish in stature, but well set and as nimble as a goat; his face was of a good open expression, but sunburnt very dark, and heavily freckled and pitted with the small-pox; his eyes were unusually light and had a kind of dancing madness in them, that was both engaging and alarming; and when he took off his great-coat, he laid a pair of fine silver-mounted pistols on the table, and I saw that he was belted with a great sword.

15 His manners, besides, were elegant, and he pledged the captain handsomely. Altogether I thought of him, at the first sight, that here was a man I would rather call my friend than my enemy.

The captain, too, was taking his observations, but rather of the man's clothes than his person. And to be sure, as soon as he had taken off the great-coat, he showed forth

20 mighty fine for the round-house of a merchant brig: having a hat with feathers, a red waistcoat, breeches of black plush, and a blue coat with silver buttons and handsome silver lace; costly clothes, though somewhat spoiled with the fog and being slept in.

"I'm vexed, sir, about the boat," says the captain.

"There are some pretty men gone to the bottom," said the stranger, " that I would rather

25 see on the dry land again than half a score of boats."

"Friends of yours?" said Hoseason.

"You have none such friends in your country," was the reply. "They would have died for me like dogs."

"Well, sir," said the captain, still watching him, "there are more men in the world than

30 boats to put them in."

"And that's true, too," cried the other, "and ye seem to be a gentleman of great penetration."

"I have been in France, sir," says the captain, so that it was plain he meant more by the words than showed upon the face of them.

35 "Well, sir," says the other, "and so has many a pretty man, for the matter of that."

MARKS

"No doubt, sir," says the captain, "and fine coats."

"Oho!" says the stranger, "is that how the wind sets?" And he laid his hand quickly on his pistols.

"Don't be hasty," said the captain. "Don't do a mischief before ye see the need of it.
40 Ye've a French soldier's coat upon your back and a Scotch tongue in your head, to be sure; but so has many an honest fellow in these days, and I dare say none the worse of it."

Questions

23. Look at paragraph 1 (lines 1—9) and summarise the circumstances of how Alan Breck Stewart came to arrive on the Covenant. You should make at least four key points.   **4**

24. Look at paragraph 2 (lines 10—17).

     In your own words, explain what David Balfour's first impressions were of Alan Breck Stewart's physical appearance and character.   **4**

25. Look at the conversation between Alan Breck Stewart and Captain Hoseason (lines 23—42).

     Show how any **two** examples of the writer's use of language contributes to the creation of tension in the dialogue.   **4**

26. With reference to this extract and to elsewhere in the novel, discuss the development of David and Alan's relationship.   **8**

[Turn over

OR

Text 4 — Prose

If you choose this text you may not attempt a question on Prose in Section 2.

Read the extract below and then attempt the following questions.

***The Telegram* by Iain Crichton Smith**

The elder had passed the Murrays. The next house was her own. She sat perfectly still. Oh, pray God it wasn't hers. And yet it must be hers. Surely it must be hers. She had dreamt of this happening, her son drowning in the Atlantic ocean, her own child whom she had reared, whom she had seen going to play football in his green jersey and white
5 shorts, whom she had seen running home from school. She could see him drowning but she couldn't make out the name of the ship. She had never seen a really big ship and what she imagined was more like the mailboat than a cruiser. Her son couldn't drown out there for no reason that she could understand. God couldn't do that to people. It was impossible. God was kinder than that. God helped you in your sore trouble. She began to
10 mutter a prayer over and over. She said it quickly like the Catholics. O God save my son O God save my son O God save my son. She was ashamed of prattling in that way as if she was counting beads but she couldn't stop herself, and on top of that she would soon cry. She knew it and she didn't want to cry in front of that woman, that foreigner. It would be weakness. She felt the arm of the thin woman around her shoulders, the thin arm and it
15 was like first love, it was like the time Murdo had taken her hand in his when they were coming home from the dance, such an innocent gesture, such a spontaneous gesture. So unexpected, so strange, so much a gift. She was crying and she couldn't look . . .

"He has passed your house," said the thin woman, in a distant firm voice, and she looked
20 up. He was walking along and he had indeed passed her house. She wanted to stand up and dance all around the kitchen, all fifteen stone of her, and shout and cry and sing a song but then she stopped. She couldn't do that. How could she do that when it must be the thin woman's son? There was no other house. The thin woman was looking out at the elder, her lips pressed closely together, white and bloodless. Where had she learnt that
25 self control? She wasn't crying or shaking. She was looking out at something she had always dreaded but she wasn't going to cry or surrender or give herself away to anyone.

And at that moment the fat woman saw. She saw the years of discipline, she remembered how thin and unfed and pale the thin woman had always looked, how sometimes she had had to borrow money, even a shilling to buy food. She saw what it must have been like to
30 be a widow bringing up a son in a village not her own. She saw it so clearly that she was astounded. It was as if she had an extra vision, as if the air itself brought the past with all its details nearer. The number of times the thin woman had been ill and people had said that she was weak and useless. She looked down at the thin woman's arm. It was so shrivelled, and dry.

35 And the elder walked on.

MARKS

Questions

27. Look closely at lines 1—18.

    How does the writer use language effectively to create tension?   4

28. Look closely at the description of the thin woman in lines 19—26.

    Show how the writer uses word choice to demonstrate:

    (*a*) her fear;   2

    (*b*) her self-control.   2

29. In your own words, summarise the main difficulties the thin woman has had to overcome in her life. You should make at least four points.   4

30. By referring to this story, and to at least one other story by Iain Crichton Smith, show how he is successful in creating a character or characters we can feel sympathy for.   8

[Turn over

OR

Text 5 — Prose

If you choose this text you may not attempt a question on Prose in Section 2.

Read the extract below and then attempt the following questions.

Away in a Manger **by Anne Donovan**

This year the nativity was bigger than life-sized. The figures were bronze statues, staunin on a carpet of straw and surrounded by what looked like a hoose made of glass. It was placed tae wan side of the square, inside a fence. Sandra thought it was quite dull lookin. Weans liked bright colours and these huge people were kind of scary. She minded the wee
5 plastic figures of Mary and Joseph she used tae set carefully in place every Christmas, leavin the baby Jesus tae last. They'd fitted intae the palm of her haund. She'd need tae get a crib for Amy. Sandra wisnae very religious, no religious at all, really, but still, it was nice for the wee ones tae have a crib.

"Is that a manger, Mammy?" Amy pointed.

10 "That's right. D'you know who all the people are?"

Amy sucked at her mitt and looked carefully at the figures. "That's Mary and that's Joseph — and that's the baby Jesus. And that's a shepherd wi his sheep. But who's that, Mammy?"

"They're the three wise kings. Look — they've got presents for the baby Jesus."

15 "But who's that, Mammy? Behind the cow."

Huddled in the straw, hidden in a corner behind the figure of a large beast, lay a man. He was slightly built, dressed in auld jeans and a thin jaicket. One of his feet stuck oot round the end of the statue and on it was a worn trainin shoe, the cheapest kind they sold in the store. Sandra moved round tae get a better look at him. He was quite young, wi a
20 pointed face and longish dark hair. A stubbly growth covered his chin. He seemed sound asleep.

"Is he an angel, Mammy?"

Sandra didnae answer. She was lookin at the glass structure wonderin how on earth he'd got in. One of the panels at the back looked a bit loose, but you'd think they'd have an
25 alarm on it. Lucky for him they never — at least he'd be warm in there. She was that intent on the glass panels that she'd nearly forgotten he wisnae a statue. Suddenly he opened his eyes. They were grey.

Amy grabbed her mother's arm and started jumpin up and down.

"Mammy, look, he's alive! Look Mammy. He's an angel!"

MARKS

Questions

31. Using your own words as far as possible, summarise the main events in this extract. You should make at least two key points.

2

32. Look at lines 1—3. The writer uses a number of techniques to show how Amy tries to makes sense of the scene. Identify two techniques and explain their effects.

4

33. Look at lines 7—8 from "Sandra wisnae...". The writer creates the impression of Sandra thinking. Choose any one aspect of the writer's use of language and explain its effect.

2

34. Look at lines 16—20. The writer uses word choice to create a detailed picture of the man. Identify **two** separate examples of the writer's word choice from these lines and comment on their effects.

4

35. With reference to this story and at least one other story by Donovan, discuss how any one theme is explored.

8

[Turn over

PART C — SCOTTISH TEXT — POETRY

Text 1 — Poetry

If you choose this text you may not attempt a question on Poetry in Section 2.

Read the poem below and then attempt the following questions.

War Photographer **by Carol Ann Duffy**

In his darkroom he is finally alone
with spools of suffering set out in ordered rows.
The only light is red and softly glows,
as though this were a church and he
5 a priest preparing to intone a Mass.
Belfast. Beirut. Phnom Penh. All flesh is grass.

He has a job to do. Solutions slop in trays
beneath his hands, which did not tremble then
though seem to now. Rural England. Home again
10 to ordinary pain which simple weather can dispel,
to fields which don't explode beneath the feet
of running children in a nightmare heat.

Something is happening. A stranger's features
faintly start to twist before his eyes,
15 a half-formed ghost. He remembers the cries
of this man's wife, how he sought approval
without words to do what someone must
and how the blood stained into foreign dust.

A hundred agonies in black and white
20 from which his editor will pick out five or six
for Sunday's supplement. The reader's eyeballs prick
with tears between the bath and pre-lunch beers.
From the aeroplane he stares impassively at where
he earns his living and they do not care.

MARKS

Questions

36. As the photographer prepares to develop the film we learn important things about him.

    Identify two important things we learn about him from stanza one.   2

37. Show how two examples of the poet's use of language in stanza two highlight the effect the photographer's work has had on the photographer.   4

38. Show how one example of the poet's use of language contributes to the dramatic effect of stanza three.   2

39. How effective do you find any two aspects of the final stanza as a conclusion to the poem?

    Your answer might deal with ideas and/or language.   4

40. Using close textual reference, show how the presentation of the main character in this poem is similar or different to the presentation of the main character in another poem or poems by Duffy which you have read.   8

[Turn over

OR

Text 2 — Poetry

If you choose this text you may not attempt a question on Poetry in Section 2.

Read the poem below and then attempt the following questions.

In the Snack-bar **by Edwin Morgan**

A cup capsizes along the formica,
slithering with a dull clatter.
A few heads turn in the crowded evening snack-bar.
An old man is trying to get to his feet
5 from the low round stool fixed to the floor.
Slowly he levers himself up, his hands have no power.
He is up as far as he can get. The dismal hump
looming over him forces his head down.
He stands in his stained beltless gabardine
10 like a monstrous animal caught in a tent
in some story. He sways slightly,
the face not seen, bent down
in shadow under his cap.
Even on his feet he is staring at the floor
15 or would be, if he could see.
I notice now his stick, once painted white
but scuffed and muddy, hanging from his right arm.
Long blind, hunchback born, half paralysed
he stands
20 fumbling with the stick
and speaks:
'I want – to go to the – toilet.'

It is down two flights of stairs but we go.
I take his arm. 'Give me – your arm – it's better,' he says.
25 Inch by inch we drift towards the stairs.
A few yards of floor are like a landscape
to be negotiated, in the slow setting out
time has almost stopped. I concentrate
my life to his: crunch of spilt sugar,
30 slidy puddle from the night's umbrellas,

table edges, people's feet,

hiss of the coffee-machine, voices and laughter,

smell of a cigar, hamburgers, wet coats steaming,

and the slow dangerous inches to the stairs.

Questions

41. (a) Identify two of the poem's main ideas or central concerns that are introduced in this extract. **2**

    (b) Show how any two examples of the poet's use of language in stanza 1 help to make these concerns clear to readers. **4**

42. Explain how the poet's own role in what is happening in the snack-bar changes from stanza 1 to stanza 2. **2**

43. Look at lines 23—34. Show how the poet uses language to emphasise the difficulty of the start of the journey to the toilet. **4**

44. By closely referring to the text of this and at least one other Morgan poem, show how Morgan uses language effectively to create interesting characters. **8**

[Turn over

OR

Text 3 — Poetry

If you choose this text you may not attempt a question on Poetry in Section 2.

Read the poem below and then attempt the following questions.

Basking Shark by Norman MacCaig

To stub an oar on a rock where none should be,
To have it rise with a slounge out of the sea
Is a thing that happened once (too often) to me.

But not too often—though enough I count as gain
5 That once I met, on a sea tin-tacked with rain,
That roomsized monster with a matchbox brain.

He displaced more than water He shoggled me
Centuries back—this decadent townee
Shook on a wrong branch of his family tree.

10 Swish up the dirt and, when it settles, a spring
Is all the clearer. I saw me, in one fling,
Emerging from the slime of everything.

So who's the monster? The thought made me grow pale
For twenty seconds while as, sail after sail,
15 The tall fin slid away, and then the tail.

MARKS

Questions

45. Look at stanza 1. What event is described in this stanza and how does MacCaig react? Refer to the poet's language in your answer.

   3

46. Referring closely to stanza 2, show how MacCaig uses word choice to convey how he feels about the encounter.

   4

47. "He displaced more than water". Explain what this line means and show how the poet in the rest of the stanza develops this idea further.

   3

48. Choose an example of word choice in stanza 4 and explain how effective you find this example.

   2

49. MacCaig often describes his personal experiences in his poetry, using these to explore wider themes. Referring closely to this poem and to at least one other poem by MacCaig, show how he uses personal experience to explore wider themes.

   8

[Turn over

OR

Text 4 — Poetry

If you choose this text you may not attempt a question on Poetry in Section 2.

Read the poem below and then attempt the following questions.

Lucozade **by Jackie Kay**

My mum is on a high bed next to sad chrysanthemums.

"Don't bring flowers, they only wilt and die."

I am scared my mum is going to die

on the bed next to the sad chrysanthemums.

5 She nods off and her eyes go back in her head.

Next to her bed is a bottle of Lucozade.

"Orange nostalgia, that's what it is," she says.

"Don't bring Lucozade, either," then fades.

"The whole day was a blur, a swarm of eyes.

10 Those doctors with their white lies.

Did you think you could cheer me up with a Woman's Own?

Don't bring magazines, too much about size."

My mum wakes up, groggy and low.

"What I want to know," she says, "is this:

15 where's the big brandy, the generous gin, the Bloody Mary,

the biscuit tin, the chocolate gingers, the dirty big meringue?"

I am sixteen; I've never tasted a Bloody Mary.

"Tell your father to bring a luxury," says she.

"Grapes have no imagination, they're just green.

20 Tell him: stop the neighbours coming."

I clear her cupboard in Ward 10B, Stobhill Hospital.

I leave, bags full, Lucozade, grapes, oranges,

sad chrysanthemums under my arms,

weighted down. I turn round, wave with her flowers.

25 My mother, on her high hospital bed, waves back.

Her face is light and radiant, dandelion hours.

Her sheets billow and whirl. She is beautiful.

Next to her the empty table is divine.

I carry the orange nostalgia home singing an old song.

Questions   MARKS

50. Look at stanzas 1 and 2 (lines 1–8).

Why does the poet's mother not want her to bring flowers or Lucozade?   **2**

51. Referring to lines 9–20, show how the poet gives the reader a clear impression of the mother's character or personality.   **4**

52. Explain how the poet uses language in lines 21–29 to indicate a clear change in the girl's feelings.   **6**

53. Identify at least one theme from this poem. Using close textual reference, show how the theme (or themes) is explored in this poem, and in at least one other poem by Jackie Kay.   **8**

[END OF SECTION 1]

[Turn over

SECTION 2 — CRITICAL ESSAY — 20 marks

Attempt ONE question from the following genres — Drama, Prose, Poetry, Film and Television Drama, or Language.

Your answer must be on a different genre from that chosen in Section 1.

You should spend approximately 45 minutes on this Section.

DRAMA

> *Answers to questions on Drama should refer to the text and to such relevant features as characterisation, key scene(s), structure, climax, theme, plot, conflict, setting . . .*

1. Choose a play in which there is a character who is important in relation to the theme of the play.

   Referring to appropriate techniques, explain how this character affects our understanding of this theme.

2. Choose a play in which there is a key scene.

   Briefly describe what happens in this scene then, by referring to dramatic techniques, go on to explain why the scene is important to the play as a whole.

PROSE

> *Answers to questions on Prose should refer to the text and to such relevant features as characterisation, setting, language, key incident(s), climax, turning point, plot, structure, narrative technique, theme, ideas, description . . .*

3. Choose a novel **or** short story **or** work of non-fiction which has a key incident.

   Give a brief account of the incident, and by referring to appropriate techniques, show how this incident is important to the text as a whole.

4. Choose a novel **or** short story in which there is a character involved in some form of conflict.

   By referring to appropriate techniques, show how the character comes to be involved in this conflict and how the conflict develops throughout the text.

POETRY

> *Answers to questions on Poetry should refer to the text and to such relevant features as word choice, tone, imagery, structure, content, rhythm, rhyme, theme, sound, ideas . . .*

5. Choose a poem which you find particularly thought-provoking.

By referring to poetic techniques, explain how the poet makes this poem so thought-provoking.

6. Choose a poem which deals with human experience.

By referring to poetic techniques, show how the poet makes this experience come alive and helps you appreciate the poem as a whole.

FILM AND TELEVISION DRAMA

> *Answers to questions on Film and Television Drama should refer to the text and to such relevant features as use of camera, key sequence, characterisation, mise-en-scène, editing, setting, music/sound, special effects, plot, dialogue . . .*

7. Choose the opening or closing scene or sequence from a film **or** television drama*.

By referring to appropriate techniques, explain why you find it an effective opening or closing scene or sequence.

8. Choose a film or television drama* which has a character who either supports or threatens the main character.

By referring to appropriate techniques, explain how this character plays an important role in the film/television drama as a whole.

* "television drama" includes a single play, a series or a serial.

[Turn over

LANGUAGE

> *Answers to questions on Language should refer to the text and to such relevant features as register, accent, dialect, slang, jargon, vocabulary, tone, abbreviation . . .*

9. Choose two advertisements, and consider the language used.

   By referring to the language techniques used, explain how effective they are at persuading you.

10. Consider the differences in language between two groups of people – for example people who live in different areas, or who have different jobs.

    By referring to appropriate language techniques, explain the main differences in language use between the two groups.

[END OF SECTION 2]

[END OF QUESTION PAPER]

National Qualifications 2015

X724/75/11

THURSDAY, 14 MAY
9:00 AM – 10:00 AM

English
Reading for Understanding, Analysis and Evaluation

Total marks — 30

Attempt ALL questions.

Write your answers clearly in the answer booklet provided. In the answer booklet you must clearly identify the question number you are attempting.

Use **blue** or **black** ink.

Before leaving the examination room you must give your answer booklet to the Invigilator; if you do not you may lose all the marks for this paper.

On the spot

If you throw a rat into the middle of a room full of humans, it will instinctively freeze. By becoming completely still, it is more likely to avoid detection. Then, it will dart into a corner of the room, hoping to flee danger. If cornered, however, it will fight. Ferociously.

5   Psychologists call it the fight-flight-freeze response, and it emerged very early in evolution. We know this because it is common to all vertebrates. The response starts in a part of the brain which reacts when an animal is confronted by a threat, and is controlled by the automatic nervous system. This is the same system that manages digestion and respiration, and is independent of conscious will.

10 At the World Cup finals, we were given a neat insight into this deeply ingrained response. The players who took penalties, and the former players who shared their experiences as pundits, talked about "the walk". This is the fearful, solitary journey from the halfway line to the penalty area in preparation for a single moment of truth: the spot-kick.

In the modern world, we rarely face danger head-on. It is not like the good old days when
15 the fight-flight-freeze response was regularly called upon to deal with predators (of both an animal and human kind). Instead, the danger we face today is artificially created: taking an exam, giving a speech, taking a penalty.

The psychological response, however, is the same. As footballers walk towards the spot, they are experiencing precisely the things you experience when put under pressure at
20 work. The threat is not to life or limb, but to ego and livelihood. We fear the consequences of messing up.

There is an acceleration of heart and lung function. There is paling and flushing. There is an inhibition of stomach action, such that digestion almost completely ceases. There is a constriction of blood vessels. There is a freeing up of metabolic energy sources (fat and
25 glycogen). There is a dilation of the pupils and a relaxation of the bladder. Perception narrows. Often, there is shaking.

All of these things are incredibly useful, in the right context. They prime the muscles; they massively increase body strength in preparation for fighting or running. The increased muscle flow and blood pressure means that you become hyper-vigilant. The
30 response is beautifully balanced for a simple reason: it helped our ancestors (and the ancestors of modern-day rats) to survive.

But there is a rather obvious problem. The fight-flight-freeze response is great for fighting, freezing or fleeing, but it is terrible if you have to do something complex, or subtle, or nuanced. When you are taking a penalty, or playing a piano concerto, or
35 marshalling the arguments necessary to pass a difficult interview, it is not helpful to have adrenalin pumping like crazy and perception obliterated by tunnel vision. You need to be calm and composed, but your body is taut, pumped and trembling.

Sports psychology can be thought of as helping performers to manage a response (ie fight, flight, freeze) that has outlived, to a large extent, its usefulness. The players standing in
40 the semi-circle holding hands are virtually motionless. It is a nice metaphor for the freeze response. The walk to the penalty spot is curiously self-conscious. You can almost hear the inner dialogue: "Get out of here, run away! 'But I can't run away. I have to take this thing!' "

How to deal with these responses? One way is with reflection. The next time you give a
45 speech or are doing a job interview, take note of how you feel. Gauge the curious feeling of dread, the desire to run away, the way your heart is beating out of your chest. But do not let this intimidate you; instead, reflect that these are normal reactions and everyone experiences them: even Michael Jordan (a marvel from the free-throw line) and Roger Federer (who always looks unnaturally calm on Centre Court).

50 One of the most creative sports psychologists has found that simply discussing the fight-flight-freeze response has huge therapeutic benefit. It takes the edge off. It makes an otherwise bewildering reaction (what on earth is going on inside me?) into a comprehensible one. To put it another way, the first stage of liberation from the tyranny of pressure is echoing the behaviour of our ancient selves.

55 This, I think, is what top athletes mean when they repeat that otherwise paradoxical saying: "Pressure is not a problem; it is a privilege". Talk to David Beckham, Sebastian Coe or Sir Chris Hoy and they will be perfectly open about their nerves and fear. But they also talk with great pride about facing up to them. They didn't see these human responses as signs of weakness but as opportunities to grow. They created mechanisms
60 (often highly personal ones) to help them through. They seized every opportunity to face danger, and learnt from each experience.

So, here is a piece of (free) advice: if you are given an opportunity to take the equivalent of a penalty, whether at work or anywhere else, grab it. Accept that you will feel uncomfortable, that your stomach will knot and that, at the moment of truth, you will
65 wish to be anywhere else in the world. Think also, as you are about to perform, of the footballers at a World Cup who volunteered to step forward with the weight of a nation's expectations on their shoulders.

Because here is the most revelatory and paradoxical thing of all: if you miss, your life will not end. If you fluff your lines, you won't die. Instead, you will grow, learn and mature.
70 And isn't that what life – whether at home, on the football pitch, or in the office – is ultimately about?

Matthew Syed, in "The Times"

Total marks — 30

Attempt ALL Questions

1. Explain fully why the first paragraph (lines 1–4) is an effective opening to the passage as a whole.

   3

2. Look at lines 5–10, and then explain **in your own words** what the writer means when he calls the response "deeply ingrained".

   2

3. Look at lines 14–21, and then explain **in your own words two** aspects of "danger" or "threat" we used to experience in the past, and **two** we face now.

   4

4. Look at lines 22–37, and then summarise, **using your own words** as far as possible, some of the changes in the body which occur with the response.

   You should make **five** key points in your answer.

   5

5. Explain why the sentence "How to deal with these responses?" (line 44) provides an appropriate link at this point in the passage.

   2

6. Look at lines 50–54, and then explain how **two** examples of the writer's **word choice** demonstrate the "benefit" of the response.

   4

7. Look at lines 55–61. Explain what the attitude of top athletes is to pressure, and how **two** examples of the language used make this attitude clear.

   5

8. Look at lines 62–67, and explain fully **using your own words** why the advice to "grab" the opportunity might at first seem strange.

   3

9. Pick an expression from the final paragraph (lines 68–71), and show how it helps to contribute to an effective conclusion to the passage.

   You should refer to an expression or idea from earlier in the article.

   2

[END OF QUESTION PAPER]

[Open out for Questions]

DO NOT WRITE ON THIS PAGE

[BLANK PAGE]

DO NOT WRITE ON THIS PAGE

National Qualifications 2015

X724/75/12

English
Critical Reading

THURSDAY, 14 MAY

10:20 AM – 11:50 AM

Total marks — 40

SECTION 1 — Scottish Text — 20 marks

Read an extract from a Scottish text you have previously studied.

Choose ONE text from either

Part A — Drama   Pages 2–7
or
Part B — Prose   Pages 8–17
or
Part C — Poetry   Pages 18–25

Attempt ALL the questions for your chosen text.

SECTION 2 — Critical Essay — 20 marks

Attempt ONE question from the following genres — Drama, Prose, Poetry, Film and Television Drama, or Language.

Your answer must be on a different genre from that chosen in Section 1.

You should spend approximately 45 minutes on each Section.

Write your answers clearly in the answer booklet provided. In the answer booklet you must clearly identify the question number you are attempting.

Use **blue** or **black** ink.

Before leaving the examination room you must give your answer booklet to the Invigilator; if you do not, you may lose all the marks for this paper.

SECTION 1 — SCOTTISH TEXT — 20 marks

PART A — SCOTTISH TEXT — DRAMA

Text 1 — Drama

If you choose this text you may not attempt a question on Drama in Section 2.

Read the extract below and then attempt the following questions.

Bold Girls by Rona Munro

Cassie and Marie are on a piece of waste ground. They are talking about their relationships with men . . .

	MARIE:	I don't know how you coped with all Joe's carry on. I don't. You were the martyr there, Cassie.
5	CASSIE:	It gave me peace.
	MARIE:	No but I couldn't have stood that, just the lying to you, the *lying* to you. I used to say to Michael, "If you go with someone else it'll tear the heart out of me but tell me, just tell me the truth 'cause I'd want to know, I couldn't bear not to know." He never did though. So I never worried.
10	CASSIE:	No.
	MARIE:	Do you know he was like my best friend. Well, sure you're my best friend but if a man can be that kind of friend to you he was to me, could tell each other anything. That's what I miss most. The crack. The *sharing*.
	CASSIE:	Marie . . .
15	MARIE:	What?
	CASSIE:	Aw Jesus I hate this place! (She gets up, kicking the ground)
	MARIE:	We'll get a weekend in Donegal again soon, the three of us and the kids. Sure we could all do with a break.
	CASSIE:	I'm leaving.
20	MARIE:	What?
		Cassie says nothing
		What do you mean you're leaving?
	CASSIE:	Do you know she gives me a tenner before every visit to go up town and buy fruit for them. "Poor Martin" and "poor Joe". That's all she's allowed to give them, all she can spoil them with, fruit, so she wants them to have grapes and melons and things you've never heard of and shapes you wouldn't know how to bite into. I'll bring her home something that looks and smells like the Botanic Gardens and she'll sniff it and stroke it like it was her favourite son himself, 'stead of his dinner . . . And I'll have three or four pounds in my pocket, saved, sure she doesn't have a clue of the price of kiwi fruit. (*Pause*) I've two hundred pounds saved. I'm going, Marie.

MARIE:	Going where?	
CASSIE:	It's desperate, isn't it? Thirty-five years old and she's stealing from her mummy's purse. Well I thought about asking the broo for a relocation grant or	

35 something you know, but it seems to me all they can offer you is the straight swap of one hell hole for another.

MARIE: You talking about a holiday?

CASSIE: I'm talking about getting out of here.

MARIE: Cassie, where could you go with two kids for two hundred pounds?

40 *Cassie says nothing for a moment*

Questions

1. Using your own words as far as possible, summarise what happens in this extract. You should make **four** key points. 4

2. Referring closely to the extract, show how **two** aspects of Marie's attitude towards men are revealed by the playwright. 4

3. By referring closely to the extract, explain **two** aspects of Cassie's mood. (You may refer to word choice, sentence structure and/or stage directions in your answer.) 4

4. Gender is an important theme in this extract. With reference to this extract and elsewhere in the play, explain how the theme of gender is explored. 8

[Turn over

OR

Text 2 — Drama

If you choose this text you may not attempt a question on Drama in Section 2.

Read the extract below and then attempt the following questions.

Sailmaker by Alan Spence

Extract from Act One

ALEC: Later on I opened the window and looked out across the back courts. The breeze was warm. Everything was the same. It was very ordinary. Nothing had changed. I don't know what I had expected. A sign. Jesus to come walking across the back and tell me everything was all right. A window in the sky to
5   open and God to lean out and say my mother had arrived safe. The sun shone on the grey tenements, on the railings and the middens, on the dustbins and the spilled ashes. It glinted on windows and on bits of broken glass. It was like something I remembered, something from a dream. Across the back, a wee boy was standing, blowing on a mouth-organ, playing the same two notes over
10   and over again.

(*Two notes on mouth organ, repeated, continuing while he talks*)

My mother was dead.

My mother was dead.

The breeze touched my cheek. It scattered the ashes round the midden. It
15   ruffled the clothes of the wee boy standing there, playing his two notes.

Over and over and over.

I looked up at the sky, the clouds moving across. Just for a minute a gap opened up, a wee patch of clear blue.

(*Two notes continuing, then fade*)

20 DAVIE: We better get this place tidied up a bit son. Folk'll be comin back after the funeral.

(*Moves around as he is talking — ALEC remains static*)

As long as ye keep movin it doesnae hit ye. Get the fire goin clean the windaes dust the furniture think about somethin for eatin don't stop keep yerself goin.
25   Sometimes for whole minutes ye can nearly *nearly* forget about it, shove it tae the back ae yer mind. Then maybe yer lookin for somethin and ye turn round tae ask her where it is an ye wonder for a minute where she's got tae and ye think she's through in the room an ye catch yerself thinkin it and it hits ye and ye think Christ this is it this is me for the rest ae ma days.

MARKS

Questions

5. Using your own words as far as possible, summarise the situation facing Alec and Davie in this extract.   **2**

6. During Alec's speech (lines 1–19), there are references to the weather and the setting. By referring closely to the text, explain how **both** of these are important in this context.   **4**

7. With close reference to **two** examples of the writer's use of language from lines 20–29, explain how Davie is coping with his situation.   **4**

8. Look closely at the language used by Alec and Davie in this extract.

   Identify **two** key differences between Alec and Davie in their use(s) of language.   **2**

9. The relationship between father and son is an important theme in the play.

   With close reference to this extract and elsewhere in the play, show how this theme is explored.   **8**

[Turn over

OR

Text 3 — Drama

If you choose this text you may not attempt a question on Drama in Section 2.

Read the extract below and then attempt the following questions.

Tally's Blood **by Ann Marie di Mambro**

In this scene Rosinella is getting Lucia ready for her Confirmation.

ROSINELLA:		You look just like a wee bride. I'm telling you this now, Lucia Ianelli, some day I'll give you a wedding, I'll give you a wedding like nobody here has ever seen before.
LUCIA:		(*Enthusiastic*) Just like yours?
5 ROSINELLA:		(*Cagey*) I didn't have much of a wedding, hen. We were awfy poor in they days.
LUCIA:		(*Sympathetic*) Oh, Auntie Rosinella.
ROSINELLA:		No, don't get me wrong. I wouldn't change your Uncle Massimo for any film star. No for Humphrey Bogart, no for Victor Mature. My faither wanted me to marry someone else, you know.
LUCIA:		(*Enjoying it*) He did not.
ROSINELLA:		(*Getting into it*) He did that. Ferdinando. He'd it all fixed up with Ferdinand's faither. He wasn't very good looking, Ferdinand, but all the girls were after him because he had a beautiful big piece of land. That's what it's all about over there, you know. The man's got to have land. So my daddy was that pleased when his daddy picked me. It was all set. Then I met your Uncle Massimo. I must have met him when he was a wean, before him and his faither moved to Scotland, but I don't remember. I'm no kidding you, Lucia, I knew the minute I looked at him that he was for me. He was that handsome.
LUCIA:		(*Disbelief*) My Uncle Massimo?
ROSINELLA:		That was before he put the weight on. And he'd much more hair then and it was shining black. Nero. Nero. Oh, Massimo! Swept me off ma feet he did. Oh hen, I shouldn't be telling you this . . .
25 LUCIA:		(*Desperate to hear the rest*) Oh no, go on, Auntie Rosinella.
ROSINELLA:		Well, I never married Ferdinand. I married your Uncle Massimo instead. That's why I didn't have much of a wedding. (*A beat: she is deciding whether to tell her or not, then does so, with glee.*) We ran away.
LUCIA:		(*Impressed*) You did not!
30 ROSINELLA:		(*Enjoying it now*) We did. You see, in Italy, where we come from anyway, if a boy and a girl stay out together all night, then they must get married. It's true. We planned it and we did it. My faither locked me in my room because I said I wasn't going to marry Ferdinand and your Uncle Massimo came with a ladder and stole me out the window.

35 LUCIA: (*Laughing*) He did not!

    ROSINELLA: Without a word of a lie, sure as God is my judge standing here. We just had to spend one night together, on our own. But we had nowhere to go so we hid up a tree. And we could hear them out looking for us, all around the village, calling our names and chapping all the doors. My daddy was 40   screaming and shouting at the top of his voice and calling me for everything. And the next morning the priest rang the bell — (*She mimics the sound*) "Do-ing, Do-ing, Do-ing" — the way he does when someone has died, to let everyone in the village know I'd disgraced my name and brought shame on my whole family. Oh it was lovely, so it was.

Questions

10. Using your own words as far as possible, summarise the story that Rosinella tells Lucia about her wedding to Massimo. You should make **four** key points.   4

11. Referring closely to the extract, explain fully how the stage directions reveal Rosinella's changing thoughts about telling Lucia this story.   4

12. Identify **one** interesting use of tone created in this extract and explain how it is created.   2

13. Even though Rosinella is Italian, her speech shows signs of her having lived in Scotland. Find **two** examples from the passage which indicate this.   2

14. By referring to this extract and to elsewhere in the play, show how the playwright explores romantic relationships.   8

[Turn over

SECTION 1 — SCOTTISH TEXT — 20 marks

PART B — SCOTTISH TEXT — PROSE

Text 1 — Prose

If you choose this text you may not attempt a question on Prose in Section 2.

Read the extract below and then attempt the following questions.

***The Cone-Gatherers* by Robin Jenkins**

In this extract, the brothers are returning to their hut, through the woods. They are being watched by the gamekeeper Duror.

While his brother was moving away shouting, Calum was kneeling by the rabbit. He had seen it done before: grip the ears firmly, stretch the neck, and strike with the side of the hand: so simple was death. But as he touched the long ears, and felt them warm and pulsating with a life not his own, he realised he could not do the rabbit this peculiar
5 kindness; he must leave it to the callous hand or boot of the gamekeeper.

He rose and ran stumbling and whimpering after his brother.

Hidden among the spruces at the edge of the ride, near enough to catch the smell of larch off the cones and to be struck by some of those thrown, stood Duror the gamekeeper, in an icy sweat of hatred, with his gun aimed all the time at the
10 feebleminded hunchback grovelling over the rabbit. To pull the trigger, requiring far less force than to break a rabbit's neck, and then to hear simultaneously the clean report of the gun and the last obscene squeal of the killed dwarf would have been for him, he thought, release too, from the noose of disgust and despair drawn, these past few days, so much tighter.

15 He had waited for over an hour there to see them pass. Every minute had been a purgatory of humiliation: it was as if he was in their service, forced to wait upon them as upon his masters. Yet he hated and despised them far more powerfully than he had liked and respected Sir Colin and Lady Runcie-Campbell. While waiting, he had imagined them in the darkness missing their footing in the tall tree and coming crashing down through
20 the sea of branches to lie dead on the ground. So passionate had been his visualising of that scene, he seemed himself to be standing on the floor of a fantastic sea, with an owl and a herd of deer flitting by as quiet as fish, while the yellow ferns and bronzen brackens at his feet gleamed like seaweed, and the spruce trees swayed above him like submarine monsters.

25 He could have named, item by item, leaf and fruit and branch, the overspreading tree of revulsion in him; but he could not tell the force which made it grow, any more than he could have explained the life in himself, or in the dying rabbit, or in any of the trees about him.

This wood had always been his stronghold and sanctuary; there were many places secret
30 to him where he had been able to fortify his sanity and hope. But now the wood was invaded and defiled; its cleansing and reviving virtues were gone. Into it had crept this hunchback, himself one of nature's freaks, whose abject acceptance of nature, like the whining prostrations of a heathen in front of an idol, had made acceptance no longer possible for Duror himself.

MARKS

Questions

15. Read lines 1–5.

    Using your own words as far as possible, explain what we learn about Calum in the opening lines of this extract.

    2

16. Read lines 7–14.

    How do any **two** examples of the writer's language convey the strength of Duror's feelings towards Calum?

    4

17. Read lines 18–28.

    Choose and comment on any **two** examples of the writer's use of imagery in these lines.

    4

18. Read lines 29–34.

    In your own words, explain how Duror's feelings about the woods have changed since the arrival of the cone-gatherers.

    2

19. With close reference to this extract and elsewhere in the novel, show how the character of Calum is presented.

    8

[Turn over

OR

Text 2 — Prose

If you choose this text you may not attempt a question on Prose in Section 2.

Read the extract below and then attempt the following questions.

The Testament of Gideon Mack by James Robertson

Nevertheless I continued to lead a double or even triple life for most of my teens. It suited me to do so. The fewer people I crossed, the easier life was. At school — outside the classroom — I could be as coarse-mouthed and broad of accent and disrespectful of authority as any of my peers, although I always remained at the edge of the crowd,
5   careful to avoid serious trouble. But in classes I kept my head down and worked. Others, who didn't have my knack of disguise, were mercilessly taunted and assaulted for being good at schoolwork. I studied hard enough to be successful, so that my teachers had no cause for complaint, but my talent for duplicity enabled me also to avoid being the victim of the bullies. Some of my more academically challenged fellow pupils even admired my
10 fraudulence: it was the kind of thing they couldn't get away with, but I could make life easier for them too by helping out with their homework. I was sleekit and cowardly, even though my name was Gideon.

At home, I maintained an air of piety. Although within myself I had abandoned my faith, I continued to go to church and be the dutiful son of the manse. My hair may have grown
15 longer, and I may have slouched in front of the TV watching *Monty Python* — in comparison with which, had he ever seen it, my father would have found *Batman* a beacon of lucidity and common sense — but that was about the extent of my revolutionary activity. I had hypocrisy down to a fine art.

And so, when my father in his systematic, post-stroke slowness began to instruct me for
20 my first Communion, when I was thirteen, I did not refuse to participate, but went through with the whole business. This was a rigorous undertaking. One of my father's jobs was to prepare others for admission to the Kirk, and indeed throughout the year a trickle of young people came to the manse for this purpose. He didn't let them off easily, I am sure, but turned his fierce eyes on them in search of the light of conviction in theirs; and
25 a few abandoned the process under his interrogation. This flushing out of the unworthy he would have reckoned almost as much of a victory as bringing the chosen few safely into the Kirk. But from his own son he required an even greater commitment.

Think of this: the 107 questions and answers of the Westminster Shorter Catechism, in all their Calvinist glory. You would have to go a long way west and north of Ochtermill in the
30 1970s to find Presbyterians who learned their Shorter Catechism by heart, but I did. I was no Calvinist, the Church of Scotland had long since paid only lip-service to the tenets of the Westminster Confession of Faith, and even my father, old-fashioned in so many ways, had moved some distance from a rigid interpretation of such ideas as election and justification. Yet he used the Catechism to educate me in the Presbyterian faith; and we
35 worked through the questions and answers much as we'd once worked through the detail of our days over the dinner table, as a kind of exercise in pigeon-holing holy information. We dissected and deciphered the nature of God, the nature of mankind, the nature of sin, the nature of faith, the requirements of the ten commandments, the form of the sacraments and the meaning of the Lord's Prayer. "What is prayer?" he would ask me, and
40 I, who had given it up months before, would say, "Prayer is an offering up of our desires to God, for things agreeable to his will, in the name of Christ, with confession of our sins, and thankful acknowledgement of his mercies," and then we would talk about

what that meant, and look at the several texts from the Bible that proved the points. And all the while, the many, many hours that this took, the apostate in me was picking holes
45 in the arguments, but saying nothing, and the voluble hypocrite was mending them. I'll say this: the grounding for the ministry I would later have at New College was less thorough than the one I had from my father in his stoury study. We understood each other better then than perhaps we ever did. I wouldn't say there was warmth between us, but there was something like mutual respect. And yet, though I was there with him, a part of
50 me was keeping its distance.

Questions

20. Look at lines 1–18. Using your own words as far as possible, explain what we learn about Gideon's character from these lines You should make **four** key points.   4

21. Look at lines 19–50.

    (a) Show how **two** examples of the writer's use of word choice makes it clear how difficult it was to learn all that was needed for the first Communion.   4

    (b) Show how **one** example of the writer's use of sentence structure makes it clear how much there was to learn.   2

22. Look at lines 44–50. Explain in your own words the effect that this tutoring has on the relationship between Gideon and his father.   2

23. Referring to this extract and elsewhere in the novel, show how the theme of deception is explored.   8

[Turn over

OR

Text 3 — Prose

If you choose this text you may not attempt a question on Prose in Section 2.

Read the extract below and then attempt the following questions.

Kidnapped by Robert Louis Stevenson

In this extract, which is from Chapter 2 of the novel, David Balfour approaches Edinburgh as he seeks out his uncle, Ebenezer Balfour, and the house of Shaws.

Presently after, I came by a house where a shepherd lived, and got a rough direction for the neighbourhood of Cramond; and so, from one to another, worked my way to the westward of the capital by Colinton, till I came out upon the Glasgow road. And there, to my great pleasure and wonder, I beheld a regiment marching to the fifes, every foot in
5 time; an old red-faced general on a grey horse at the one end, and at the other the company of Grenadiers, with their Pope's-hats. The pride of life seemed to mount into my brain at the sight of the redcoats and the hearing of that merry music.

A little farther on, and I was told I was in Cramond parish, and began to substitute in my inquiries the name of the house of Shaws. It was a word that seemed to surprise those of
10 whom I sought my way. At first I thought the plainness of my appearance, in my country habit, and that all dusty from the road, consorted ill with the greatness of the place to which I was bound. But after two, or maybe three, had given me the same look and the same answer, I began to take it in my head there was something strange about the Shaws itself.

15 The better to set this fear at rest, I changed the form of my inquiries; and spying an honest fellow coming along a lane on the shaft of his cart, I asked him if he had ever heard tell of a house they called the house of Shaws.

He stopped his cart and looked at me, like the others.

"Ay," said he. "What for?"

20 "It's a great house?" I asked.

"Doubtless," says he. "The house is a big, muckle house."

"Ay," said I, "but the folk that are in it?"

"Folk?" cried he. "Are ye daft? There's nae folk there — to call folk."

"What?" say I; "not Mr. Ebenezer?"

25 "Oh, ay," says the man, "there's the laird, to be sure, if it's him you're wanting. What'll like be your business, mannie?"

"I was led to think that I would get a situation," I said, looking as modest as I could.

"What?" cries the carter, in so sharp a note that his very horse started; and then, "Well, mannie," he added, "it's nane of my affairs; but ye seem a decent-spoken lad; and if ye'll
30 take a word from me, ye'll keep clear of the Shaws."

The next person I came across was a dapper little man in a beautiful white wig, whom I saw to be a barber on his rounds; and knowing well that barbers were great gossips, I asked him plainly what sort of a man was Mr Balfour of the Shaws.

"Hoot, hoot, hoot," said the barber, "nae kind of a man, nae kind of a man at all"; and
35 began to ask me very shrewdly what my business was; but I was more than a match for
him at that, and he went on to his next customer no wiser than he came.

I cannot well describe the blow this dealt to my illusions. The more indistinct the
accusations were, the less I liked them, for they left the wider field to fancy. What kind
of a great house was this, that all the parish should start and stare to be asked the way to
40 it? or what sort of a gentleman, that his ill-fame should be thus current on the wayside?

Questions

24. Using your own words as far as possible, summarise what happens in this extract
from the novel. Make at least **four** key points.   4

25. Look at lines 8—12 ("A little farther on . . . place to which I was bound.").

    Initially, why did David feel he was "surprising" people with his inquiries about
    directions to the house of Shaws? You should answer in your own words as far as
    possible.   2

26. By referring to an example of the writer's language, explain how the writer
    effectively highlights David's mood:

    (a) at the start of the extract (lines 1—7);   3

    (b) at the end of the extract (lines 37—40).   3

27. By referring to this extract and to elsewhere in the novel, show how the character
    of David Balfour is developed.   8

[Turn over

OR

Text 4 — Prose

If you choose this text you may not attempt a question on Prose in Section 2.

Read the extract below and then attempt the following questions.

Mother and Son by Iain Crichton Smith

His mind now seemed gradually to be clearing up, and he was beginning to judge his own actions and hers. Everything was clearing up: it was one of his moments. He turned round on his chair from a sudden impulse and looked at her intensely. He had done this very often before, had tried to cow her into submission: but she had always laughed at him.
5 Now however he was looking at her as if he had never seen her before. Her mouth was open and there were little crumbs upon her lower lip. Her face had sharpened itself into a birdlike quickness: she seemed to be pecking at the bread with a sharp beak in the same way as she pecked cruelly at his defences. He found himself considering her as if she were some kind of animal. Detachedly he thought: how can this thing make my life a
10 hell for me? What is she anyway? She's been ill for ten years: that doesn't excuse her. She's breaking me up so that even if she dies I won't be any good for anyone. But what if she's pretending? What if there is nothing wrong with her? At this a rage shook him so great that he flung his half-consumed cigarette in the direction of the fire in an abrupt, savage gesture. Out of the silence he heard a bus roaring past the window, splashing over
15 the puddles. That would be the boys going to town to enjoy themselves. He shivered inside his loneliness and then rage took hold of him again. How he hated her! This time his gaze concentrated itself on her scraggy neck, rising like a hen's out of her plain white nightgown. He watched her chin wagging up and down: it was stained with jam and flecked with one or two crumbs. His sense of loneliness closed round him, so that he felt
20 as if he were on a boat on the limitless ocean, just as his house was on a limitless moorland. There was a calm, unspeaking silence, while the rain beat like a benediction on the roof. He walked over to the bed, took the tray from her as she held it out to him. He had gone in answer to words which he hadn't heard, so hedged was he in his own thoughts.

25 "Remember to clean the tray tomorrow," she said. He walked back with the tray fighting back the anger that swept over him carrying the rubbish and debris of his mind in its wake. He turned back to the bed. His mind was in a turmoil of hate, so that he wanted to smash the cup, smash the furniture, smash the house. He kept his hands clenched, he the puny and unimaginative. He would show her, avenge her insults with his unintelligent
30 hands. There was the bed, there was his mother. He walked over.

MARKS

Questions

28. From this extract, summarise in your own words as far as possible, the main reasons for John's anger towards his mother. You should make at least **four** key points.

4

29. Look closely at lines 5—14 ("Now however . . . savage gesture.").

Show how any **two** examples of the writer's use of language contribute to our understanding of John's feelings towards his mother.

4

30. With close reference to lines 14—24 ("Out of . . . his own thoughts."), show how the writer uses language effectively to emphasise John's feelings of loneliness.

2

31. Look at lines 25—30. With reference to **one** example of the writer's use of language, explain how tension is created.

2

32. With close reference to this extract and at least one other story by Ian Crichton Smith, show how a character comes to realise something of importance.

8

[Turn over

OR

Text 5 — Prose

If you choose this text you may not attempt a question on Prose in Section 2.

Read the extract below and then attempt the following questions.

All That Glisters **by Anne Donovan**

The funeral wis on the Wednesday and the days in between were a blur of folk comin an goin, of makin sandwiches an drinkin mugs of stewed tea, sayin rosaries an pourin oot glasses of whisky for men in overcoats. His body came hame tae the hoose and wis pit in their bedroom. Ma mammy slept in the bed settee in the livin room wi ma Auntie Pauline.

5   *Are you sure that you want tae see him?*

    Ah wis sure. Ah couldnae bear the fact we'd never said goodbye and kept goin ower and ower in ma mind whit ah'd have said tae him if ah'd known he wis gonnae die so soon. Ah wis feart as well, right enough. Ah'd never seen a deid body afore, and ah didnae know whit tae expect, but he looked as if he wis asleep, better in fact than he'd
10 looked when he wis alive, his face had mair colour, wis less yella lookin an lined. Ah sat wi him fur a while in the room, no sayin anything, no even thinkin really, just sittin. Ah felt that his goin wis incomplete and ah wanted tae dae sumpn fur him, but that's daft, whit can you dae when sumbdy's deid? Ah wondered if ah should ask ma mammy but she wis that withdrawn intae hersel, so busy wi the arrangements that ah didnae like tae. She
15 still smiled at me but it wis a watery far-away smile and when she kissed me goodnight ah felt she wis haudin me away fae her.

    On the Wednesday mornin ah got up early, got dressed and went through tae the kitchen. Ma Auntie Pauline wis sittin at the table havin a cuppa tea and a fag and when she looked up her face froze over.

20   *Whit the hell dae you think you're daein? Go and get changed this minute.*

    But these are ma best claes.

    You cannae wear red tae a funeral. You have tae show respect fur the deid.

    But these were ma daddy's favourites. He said ah looked brilliant in this.

    Ah mind his face when ah came intae the room a couple of month ago, after ma
25 mammy'd bought me this outfit fur ma birthday; a red skirt and a zip-up jaicket wi red tights tae match.

    You're a sight fur sore eyes, hen.

    That sounds horrible, daddy.

    He smiled at me.

30   *It disnae mean that, hen, it means you look that nice that you would make sore eyes feel better. Gie's a twirl, princess.*

    And ah birled roon on wan leg, laughin.

MARKS

Questions

33. Using your own words as far as possible, summarise what happens in this extract. You should make **four** key points.   4

34. Look at lines 1—3. Explain how the writer uses language to convey the memory of the days before the funeral. You should refer to **two** examples in your answer.   4

35. Look at lines 6—16. Identify **two** ways in which the writer develops a strong sense of narrative voice at this point in the extract.   2

36. Look at lines 17—23. By referring to **one** example, explain fully how the aunt's reaction is shown.   2

37. By referring closely to this extract and to at least one other story by Donovan, show how the theme of relationships is developed.   8

[Turn over

SECTION 1 — SCOTTISH TEXT — 20 marks

PART C — SCOTTISH TEXT — POETRY

Text 1 — Poetry

If you choose this text you may not attempt a question on Poetry in Section 2.

Read the poem below and then attempt the following questions.

Valentine **by Carol Ann Duffy**

Not a red rose or a satin heart.

I give you an onion.
It is a moon wrapped in brown paper.
It promises light
5 like the careful undressing of love.

Here.
It will blind you with tears
like a lover.
It will make your reflection
10 a wobbling photo of grief.

I am trying to be truthful.

Not a cute card or a kissogram.

I give you an onion.
Its fierce kiss will stay on your lips,
15 possessive and faithful
as we are,
for as long as we are.

Take it.
Its platinum loops shrink to a wedding ring,
20 if you like.
Lethal.
Its scent will cling to your fingers,
cling to your knife.

MARKS

Questions

38. In the opening two lines of the poem some of the main ideas and concerns of the poem come across clearly. Identify **two** of these main ideas or concerns.

2

39. In lines 3–5, show how **two** examples of the poet's use of language suggest a positive side to love.

4

40. In lines 7–17, show how **two** examples of the poet's use of language suggest a negative side to love.

4

41. How effective do you find lines 18–23 as a conclusion to the poem?

Justify your answer with close reference to the text.

2

42. The theme of relationships is important in this poem. With close textual reference, show how this theme is explored in this poem and in at least one other poem you have read by Duffy.

8

[Turn over

OR

Text 2 — Poetry

If you choose this text you may not attempt a question on Poetry in Section 2.

Read the poem below and then attempt the following questions.

Hyena **by Edwin Morgan**

I am waiting for you.
I have been travelling all morning through the bush
and not eaten.
I am lying at the edge of the bush
5 on a dusty path that leads from the burnt-out kraal.
I am panting, it is midday, I found no water-hole.
I am very fierce without food and although my eyes
are screwed to slits against the sun
you must believe I am prepared to spring.

10 What do you think of me?
I have a rough coat like Africa.
I am crafty with dark spots
like the bush-tufted plains of Africa.
I sprawl as a shaggy bundle of gathered energy
15 like Africa sprawling in its waters.
I trot, I lope, I slaver, I am a ranger.
I hunch my shoulders. I eat the dead.

Do you like my song?
When the moon pours hard and cold on the veldt
20 I sing, and I am the slave of darkness.
Over the stone walls and the mud walls and the ruined places
and the owls, the moonlight falls.
I sniff a broken drum. I bristle. My pelt is silver.
I howl my song to the moon — up it goes.
25 Would you meet me there in the waste places?

It is said I am a good match
for a dead lion. I put my muzzle
at his golden flanks, and tear. He
is my golden supper, but my tastes are easy.
30 I have a crowd of fangs, and I use them.
Oh and my tongue — do you like me
when it comes lolling out over my jaw
very long, and I am laughing?
I am not laughing.
35 But I am not snarling either, only
panting in the sun, showing you
what I grip
carrion with.

MARKS

I am waiting
40 for the foot to slide,
for the heart to seize,
for the leaping sinews to go slack,
for the fight to the death to be fought to the death,
for a glazing eye and the rumour of blood.
45 I am crouching in my dry shadows
till you are ready for me.
My place is to pick you clean
and leave your bones to the wind.

Questions

43. Using your own words as far as possible, identify **two** things which you learn about the hyena in stanza one (lines 1—9).

2

44. Explain fully how **two** examples of the poet's use of language in stanza two (lines 10—17) increase your understanding of the hyena.

4

45. By referring closely to **two** examples from stanzas 3 and 4 (lines 18—38), show how the writer uses language to develop a tense, menacing atmosphere.

4

46. How effective do you find the last stanza (lines 39—48) as a conclusion to the poem? Justify your answer with close reference to the text.

2

47. By referring closely to this poem, and to at least **one** other poem by Morgan, show how the writer uses word choice and/or imagery effectively to create a striking visual impression, or scene.

8

[Turn over

OR

Text 3 — Poetry

If you choose this text you may not attempt a question on Poetry in Section 2.

Read the poem below and then attempt the following questions.

Visiting Hour **by Norman MacCaig**

The hospital smell
combs my nostrils
as they go bobbing along
green and yellow corridors.

5 What seems a corpse
is trundled into a lift and vanishes
heavenward.

I will not feel, I will not
feel, until
10 I have to.

Nurses walk lightly, swiftly,
here and up and down and there,
their slender waists miraculously
carrying their burden
15 of so much pain, so
many deaths, their eyes
still clear after
so many farewells.

Ward 7. She lies
20 in a white cave of forgetfulness.
A withered hand
trembles on its stalk. Eyes move
behind eyelids too heavy
to raise. Into an arm wasted
25 of colour a glass fang is fixed,
not guzzling but giving.
And between her and me
distance shrinks till there is none left
but the distance of pain that neither she nor I
30 can cross.

She smiles a little at this
black figure in her white cave
who clumsily rises
in the round swimming waves of a bell
35 and dizzily goes off, growing fainter,
not smaller, leaving behind only
books that will not be read
and fruitless fruits.

MARKS

Questions

48. Look at lines 1–10. Show how MacCaig feels about his hospital visit, referring to **two** examples of language.

    4

49. Look at lines 11–18. Referring to **two** examples, explain how MacCaig uses poetic techniques to reveal his attitude towards the nurses.

    4

50. Look at lines 19–30. By referring to **two** examples of the poet's use of language, explain how he makes clear the patient's condition.

    4

51. MacCaig often uses imagery in his poems. Referring closely to this poem and at least one other poem by MacCaig, show how he uses imagery effectively.

    8

[Turn over

OR

Text 4 — Poetry

If you choose this text you may not attempt a question on Poetry in Section 2.

Read the poem below and then attempt the following questions.

***Divorce* by Jackie Kay**

I did not promise
to stay with you til death do us part, or
anything like that,
so part I must, and quickly. There are things
5 I cannot suffer
any longer: Mother, you never, ever said
a kind word
or a thank-you for all the tedious chores I have done;
Father, your breath
10 smells like a camel's and gives me the hump;
all you ever say is:
"Are you off in the cream puff, Lady Muck?"
In this day and age?
I would be better off in an orphanage.

15 I want a divorce.
There are parents in the world whose faces turn
up to the light
who speak in the soft murmur of rivers
and never shout.
20 There are parents who stroke their children's cheeks
in the dead of night
and sing in the colourful voices of rainbows,
red to blue.
These parents are not you. I never chose you.
25 You are rough and wild,
I don't want to be your child. All you do is shout
And that's not right.
I will file for divorce in the morning at first light.

MARKS

Questions

52. How does the speaker make it clear that she wants to separate herself from her parents in the first sentence of the poem (lines 1—4)? You may refer to language or ideas in your answer.

2

53. Using your own words as far as possible, summarise the impression the speaker gives of her parents in lines 1—14. You should make **three** clear points in your answer.

3

54. Look at lines 16—23. Explain, with reference to **two** examples of the poet's language, how she makes clear how she imagines other parents to be.

4

55. The poet uses different tones throughout the poem. Identify any **one** use of tone and, by making reference to the text, show how the tone is created.

3

56. With close textual reference, show how the theme of family relationships is explored in this poem, and in at least one other poem by Jackie Kay.

8

[END OF SECTION 1]

[Turn over

SECTION 2 — CRITICAL ESSAY — 20 marks

Attempt ONE question from the following genres — Drama, Prose, Poetry, Film and Television Drama, or Language.

Your answer must be on a different genre from that chosen in Section 1.

You should spend approximately 45 minutes on this Section.

DRAMA

Answers to questions on Drama should refer to the text and to such relevant features as characterisation, key scene(s), structure, climax, theme, plot, conflict, setting . . .

1. Choose a play in which an important character is in conflict with another character or characters in the play, or with herself or himself.

   Describe the conflict and then, by referring to appropriate techniques, go on to explain why the conflict is important to the development of the play as a whole.

2. Choose a play where the playwright explores a theme or issue or concern which you feel is important.

   By referring to appropriate techniques, show how effectively the playwright establishes and explores the theme or issue or concern.

PROSE

Answers to questions on Prose should refer to the text and to such relevant features as characterisation, setting, language, key incident(s), climax, turning point, plot, structure, narrative technique, theme, ideas, description . . .

3. Choose a novel **or** short story in which the writer creates a realistic or convincing character.

   By referring to appropriate techniques, show how the writer creates this character, and say why you find him or her to be realistic or convincing.

4. Choose a novel **or** short story **or** a work of non-fiction which explores a theme which you find interesting.

   By referring to appropriate techniques, show how the writer explores this theme.

POETRY

> Answers to questions on Poetry should refer to the text and to such relevant features as word choice, tone, imagery, structure, content, rhythm, rhyme, theme, sound, ideas . . .

5. Choose a poem in which setting is an important feature.

   By referring to poetic techniques, show how setting contributes to your appreciation of the poem as a whole.

6. Choose a poem which makes you think more deeply about an aspect of life.

   By referring to poetic techniques, show how the poet explores this aspect of life.

FILM AND TELEVISION DRAMA

> Answers to questions on Film and Television Drama should refer to the text and to such relevant features as use of camera, key sequence, characterisation, mise-en-scène, editing, setting, music/sound, special effects, plot, dialogue . . .

7. Choose a scene or sequence from a film **or** television drama* which creates a particular feeling or emotion.

   By referring to appropriate techniques, explain how the director leads you to feel this way.

8. Choose a film **or** television drama* which has a character who is admirable and/or unpleasant.

   By referring to appropriate techniques, explain how the character is presented in the film/television drama* as a whole.

* "television drama" includes a single play, a series or a serial.

[Turn over

LANGUAGE

> *Answers to questions on Language should refer to the text and to such relevant features as register, accent, dialect, slang, jargon, vocabulary, tone, abbreviation . . .*

9. Choose an advertisement which aims to persuade you to buy something or to change your behaviour.

    By referring to specific examples, explain how successful the persuasive language is.

10. Consider the differences in spoken or written language between two groups of people who are from different places, or who are different in significant ways.

    By referring to appropriate techniques, explain and evaluate the differences in language use.

[END OF SECTION 2]

[END OF QUESTION PAPER]

NATIONAL 5

2016

National
Qualifications
2016

X724/75/11

English
Reading for Understanding,
Analysis and Evaluation

THURSDAY, 5 MAY
1:00 PM – 2:00 PM

Total marks — 30

Attempt ALL questions.

Write your answers clearly in the answer booklet provided. In the answer booklet you must clearly identify the question number you are attempting.

Use **blue** or **black** ink.

Before leaving the examination room you must give your answer booklet to the Invigilator; if you do not you may lose all the marks for this paper.

Can Idina Menzel ever Let It Go?

When the organisers of the 2015 Super Bowl were looking for someone to follow in the footsteps of Diana Ross and Whitney Houston and belt out *The Star-Spangled Banner* in front of a global audience of 160 million, it's not hard to see why they chose Idina Menzel.

5   As the voice of Elsa the ice queen in *Frozen*, the most successful animated film of all time, who sang its ubiquitous Oscar-winning *Let It Go* (more than three million copies sold in America alone), she has a more than passing acquaintance with anthems.

The stratospheric success of *Frozen* — with takings of more than £800 million, it's No 5 in the all-time list of highest-grossing films — has elevated her into a new league.

Now she releases hit Christmas albums, has Broadway shows written for her, tours the
10   world's mega-domes and is having a TV sitcom developed.

Frozen isn't going away, either. She's spoken in the past about the much-mooted sequel but she has clearly been reprimanded by the Disney suits: "Apparently I spoke out of turn. I just assumed that because it was so successful there'd be a sequel, but Disney doesn't have sequels, so it would be a first if there was one."

15   How about the *Frozen* stage show, also much mooted? "I think they're working on that but the Disney people keep things close to their chests." If it happens, would she like to be in it? "Sure, I'd love to. But musicals take years and I'd have to play Elsa's mother, probably!"

What's definitely happening is a six-minute short, *Frozen Fever*, in which Elsa's powers threaten to scupper the birthday of her sister, Anna. "It's fun, really clever," Menzel says.
20   "There's a new song. It's pretty much a group number though." She sounds slightly disappointed.

Frozen Fever did delight both fans and Disney — it was shown in cinemas before Disney's live-action *Cinderella*, which doubtless enjoyed a mighty bump as a result. The studio may be tight-lipped about *Frozen* sequels, but they're certainly happy to milk the
25   commercial opportunities of their icy behemoth.

Whether there is a *Frozen 2* or not, Menzel is now a big star, there to be shot at. When she performed *Let It Go* in Times Square in New York on New Year's Eve she was criticised for failing to hit a high note (to be fair, she was singing in sub-zero temperatures). And though her powerful, stately turn at the Super Bowl received strong reviews, there were
30   still some who noticed the odd flat note.

The unnerving proximity of several dozen hulking American footballers may have had something to do with that. Talking about the time that she sang at the All-Star baseball game, Menzel says: "One thing I underestimated is what a strong presence these athletes have when they're standing on the line right in front of you. They're huge, standing
35   there, and you're this one woman, singing on her own. You forget about the world and the rest of the stadium because they're so . . . daunting."

One woman opposite a squad of men: it's a pertinent image given her associations with *Frozen*, a film that has regularly been touted as a feminist breakthrough. The first Disney animation to be directed (well, co-directed) by a woman, Jennifer Lee, it's quietly
40   revolutionary because, as Menzel says, "the purest love that's being celebrated is between two sisters and not because some Prince Charming is saving the day".

Yes, the two heroines are still doe-eyed and partial to shiny dresses, but their relationship is subtle: Elsa, the conflicted snow sorceress struggling to control her powers; Anna, the devoted younger sister whom she keeps at a distance for fear of turning her into a
45   popsicle. With her grandiose sulks, Elsa has been described as Disney's first emo princess. "She's definitely complicated," Menzel says. "I think that's why it's a successful film, because both women are not stereotypes."

There are parallels with Menzel's own life: she and her younger sister, Cara, had their fair share of "Do you wanna build a snowman?" moments. "She would probably tell you she
50   looks up to me, a lot," Menzel says, rather wincingly.

When *Let It Go* was nominated for Best Song at the Oscars a year ago, it was Cara whom Menzel took as her date. "I didn't think about it — she was the first person I thought of — and then I realised how perfect it was," she says. Sisters representing a film about sisters.

55   *Let It Go* won the Oscar for its writers, but that was rather overshadowed by the moment of weirdness earlier in the evening when, introducing Menzel's performance of the song, John Travolta inexplicably referred to her as "Adele Dazeem".

She nevertheless recognises that Travolta's slip was "one of the greatest mistakes ever — it helped my career, that's for sure." It's one of several references Menzel makes
60   to her career: her conversation is a mix of Broadway-speak ("I try to sing from the heart") and battle-hardened ambition.

She is certainly aware of the value of appearing in "several zeitgeist-y things across different generations: from *Rent* to *Wicked*, *Glee* to *Frozen*". There's a 'through line' between those four, she thinks: they all resonate with young people and "people who are
65   trying to find themselves. I'm proud of that. I'm not sure why that's become the pattern for me — maybe it's because I have as much to learn myself".

Our time is almost up. I'm allowed to ask one more (burning) question. Does she have her own Elsa dress, the must-have wardrobe item for girls across the western world? "No I do not!" she laughs.

70   So she doesn't ever have the urge to indulge her inner ice queen and don the full regalia? "Nah, I don't look that good as a blonde. The waistline, though — that would be fun." Part of me suspects that she'd also quite enjoy ruling over her own wintry kingdom.

Ed Potton, in "The Times"

MARKS

Total marks — 30

Attempt ALL Questions

1. Look at lines 1-6, and then explain **in your own words** why the organisers of the Super Bowl chose Idina Menzel to perform there.

    2

2. Look at lines 7-8, and then, by referring to **one** example, explain fully how the writer's use of language makes it clear that Frozen is successful.

    2

3. Look at lines 11-25, and then identify, **using your own words** as far as possible, **five** things we learn here about the Disney organisation.

    5

4. Look at lines 26-36, and then explain fully how the writer's use of language makes it clear that coping with performing under these circumstances is not easy. You should refer to **two** examples in your answer.

    4

5. By referring to the sentence in lines 37-38, explain how it helps to provide a link between the writer's ideas at this point in the passage.

    2

6. Look at lines 42-47, and then explain fully how **two** examples of the writer's **word choice** make it clear that Elsa is not just "doe-eyed and partial to shiny dresses".

    4

7. Look at lines 51-61, and then explain fully **in your own words** as far as possible why the Oscar evening was so memorable or such a success for Idina Menzel.

    2

8. Look at lines 62-69, by referring to **two** examples, explain fully how the writer makes effective use of contrast in these paragraphs. You could refer to sentence structure, tone or word choice.

    4

9. Throughout the passage, we are given information and clues about Idina Menzel's personality.

    Using your own words as far as possible, identify **five** things that we learn about her personality from the passage.

    5

[END OF QUESTION PAPER]

Page five

OPEN OUT FOR QUESTIONS

DO NOT WRITE ON THIS PAGE

[BLANK PAGE]

DO NOT WRITE ON THIS PAGE

National Qualifications 2016

English
Critical Reading

THURSDAY, 5 MAY
2:20 PM – 3:50 PM

Total marks — 40

SECTION 1 — Scottish Text — 20 marks

Read an extract from a Scottish text you have previously studied.

Choose ONE text from either

Part A — Drama   Pages 2–7
or
Part B — Prose   Pages 8–17
or
Part C — Poetry   Pages 18–25

Attempt ALL the questions for your chosen text.

SECTION 2 — Critical Essay — 20 marks

Attempt ONE question from the following genres — Drama, Prose, Poetry, Film and Television Drama, or Language.

Your answer must be on a different genre from that chosen in Section 1.

You should spend approximately 45 minutes on each Section.

Write your answers clearly in the answer booklet provided. In the answer booklet you must clearly identify the question number you are attempting.

Use **blue** or **black** ink.

Before leaving the examination room you must give your answer booklet to the Invigilator; if you do not, you may lose all the marks for this paper.

SECTION 1 — SCOTTISH TEXT — 20 marks

PART A — SCOTTISH TEXT — DRAMA

Text 1 — Drama

If you choose this text you may not attempt a question on Drama in Section 2.

Read the extract below and then attempt the following questions.

Bold Girls by Rona Munro

Extract from Scene Four (Marie and Deirdre are in Marie's house . . .)

DEIRDRE: But you'd know. I know you'd look at me and you'd be sure.

Marie doesn't turn

Deirdre gets up and clumsily pulls off her top, drags off the jeans. There are bruises all over her back. She goes to Marie and pushes the clothes in front of her
5

Here, that's you got everything back.

Marie turns, startled, then starts to laugh, hysterically. Deirdre hurls the clothes at her. She snatches the knife out of the chair and waves the blade at Marie. She advances on her slowly

I want the truth out of you. I mean it.
10

Marie backs off a step

Tell me!

Suddenly Marie flies at her

MARIE: Tell you! I'll tell you!

She wrenches the knife and the picture off the startled Deirdre and smashes and slashes Michael's picture with swift, efficient destructiveness. She looks down at the pieces at her feet for a long moment. She drops the knife on top of them. Her breathing slows. She goes to the kitchen area and comes back with a half-filled rubbish sack and some newspaper. She kneels down and starts to clear up the pieces of the picture
15

20

(Quietly) Watch your feet on that glass there. *(She wraps the glass and the shredded picture in the newspaper. She wraps the knife as well. She drops both in the rubbish sack and takes it back to the kitchen)*

Deirdre has barely moved through all of this, she watches Marie tearfully

Marie returns from the kitchen, wiping her hands
25

(Still quietly) There. *(She looks at Deirdre)* Those are some bruises you've got.

Marie reaches out and touches Deirdre's shoulder

Deirdre flinches, then allows the touch

Marie turns her gently. She looks at her bruised body. Marie touches Deirdre's back
30

Page two

MARIE:　Who did this to you?

DEIRDRE:　Just the fella she's got living with her just now.

MARIE:　(*Stroking Deirdre's back*)　They took the lying head off Michael, didn't you know? Didn't they tell you that story?

35　DEIRDRE:　(*Quietly*) Yes. (*She pulls away from Marie*)

　　　　Marie seems to focus on her again

MARIE:　Ah God forgive me . . . (*She sways momentarily. She runs her hands over her face*) You should go home. It's late.

　　　　Deirdre doesn't move

40　　　　Here. (*She offers the clothes again*)

　　　　Deirdre shakes her head again

Questions

1. Using your own words as far as possible, summarise what happens in this extract. You should make **three** key points.　　**3**

2. Look at the stage directions in lines 1–13.

   By referring to **two** examples, show how the playwright reveals that Marie is emotional in this part of the scene.　　**4**

3. Look at lines 15–23.

   Identify **one** of Marie's actions and go on to explain in your own words why this action is surprising.　　**2**

4. Think about Deirdre's attitude towards Marie in this extract.

   Identify any aspect of Deirdre's attitude and by referring to **one** example of her dialogue, explain fully how the playwright conveys this aspect of Deirdre's attitude towards Marie.　　**3**

5. There are many examples of conflict in this play. By referring to this extract and to elsewhere in the play, show how conflict is an important feature of the play.　　**8**

[Turn over

OR

Text 2 — Drama

If you choose this text you may not attempt a question on Drama in Section 2.

Read the extract below and then attempt the following questions.

Sailmaker by Alan Spence

ALEC:	How come ye chucked yer trade?
DAVIE:	It chucked me! The chandlers ah worked for shut doon. Ah got laid off. That was it. Nothin else doin. Nae work. Naebody needs sailmakers these days.
ALEC:	(*Holds up yacht*) Could ye make me a sail for this? Ah found it in the Glory Hole tae. Ah thought ye could fix it up.
DAVIE:	Oh aye. It's a beauty, eh? Be nice, aw rigged out.
	Can sail it in the park.
	Course, it'll take time. Materials'll be dear. But ah'll see what ah can do.
ALEC:	When?
DAVIE:	Wait and see. (*Hands back yacht*) Who knows? Maybe ma coupon'll come up this week!
ALEC:	Remember the last time ye won?
DAVIE:	First dividend. Two quid!
	Ah didnae let it go tae ma head mind! Didnae chuck ma job. Didnae buy a villa in the south of France. Ah think every second game was a draw that week! Never mind. Some ae these days.
	(*DAVIE sits down, takes newspaper and scrap of paper from his briefcase, writes*)
	Ah didnae bring in anythin for tea. D'ye fancy nippin doon tae the chippy, gettin a coupla fish suppers?
ALEC:	Awright.
	(*DAVIE hands him money*)
	Can ah get a pickle?
DAVIE:	Get anythin ye like. Here's somethin else ye can do for me.
	Themorra at dinnertime. Take this line to the bookie.
ALEC:	Och da!
DAVIE:	Whit's the matter?
ALEC:	It's just that . . . ah don't like that bookie. He's creepy.
DAVIE:	Away ye go!
ALEC:	An that back close where he has his pitch is aw horrible an smelly.

Page four

MARKS

30 DAVIE: (*Waves his line*) But this could be worth a fortune! Three doubles, a treble, an accumulator. If it comes up we're laughin.

Here son, ah'll leave it here wi the money inside it.

ALEC: (*Picks up line, reads it*) Why d'ye always write Mainsail at the bottom ae yer line?

35 DAVIE: That's what ye call a nom-de-plume. The bettin's illegal ye see. The bookie gets done fae time tae time. An if you put yer real name on the line, the polis might book you as well. So ye use a made-up name.

ALEC: Mainsail.

Questions

6. Using your own words as far as possible, explain how Davie is shown to be struggling in his role as a father throughout this extract. You should make **four** key points.   4

7. Look at lines 2–3 and lines 10–16.

By referring to **two** examples from these lines, show how different aspects of Davie's mood are revealed by the playwright.   4

8. Look at lines 33–38.

(a) Using your own words as far as possible, explain why Davie needed to use a false name (nom-de-plume).   2

(b) Explain what **two** things Davie's choice of false name (nom-de-plume) reveals about him.   2

9. By referring to this extract and to elsewhere in the play, show how the yacht is used as an important symbol.   8

[Turn over

OR

Text 3 — Drama

If you choose this text you may not attempt a question on Drama in Section 2.

Read the extract below and then attempt the following questions.

Tally's Blood **by Ann Marie di Mambro**

BRIDGET:	I knew you'd try to split them up. I warned our Hughie, but I never knew the lengths you'd go to.	
ROSINELLA:	What you talking about?	
BRIDGET:	You sent her back, didn't you? Didn't care who gets hurt. After all these years you sent her away.	
ROSINELLA:	Who?	
BRIDGET:	Lucia. Who else?	
ROSINELLA:	Send Lucia away? Me?	
BRIDGET:	Well, you did it to me, but you're no getting doing it to my brother.	
ROSINELLA:	I don't want to hear any more. What did I ever do to you?	
BRIDGET:	What did you do to me? You told me Franco didn't love me. You made me believe I was nothing to him — just a wee Scottish tart for him to practise on.	
ROSINELLA:	In God's name, Bridget, that's all in the past.	
BRIDGET:	To you maybe. But there's no a day goes past that it's no with me. Franco loved me. Franco loved me.	
ROSINELLA:	Franco's dead — and may God forgive you, lady, for dragging his name through the mud.	

5

10

15

This remark knocks BRIDGET off her guard and ROSINELLA gathers her strength.

20

ROSINELLA:	Now, I didn't want this fight with you, and I don't have to explain nothing to you. But just you hear this. I didn't send Lucia away, I could just as easily tear out my own heart. But I'm no sorry she's away from your brother. I cannie deny it. No harm to the boy. I've nothing against him. OK? Now that's it finished. We'll forget this conversation ever took place.	
BRIDGET:	As easy as that.	
ROSINELLA:	Yes.	
BRIDGET:	All forgotten.	
ROSINELLA:	I'll never mention it again.	
BRIDGET:	If you knew the damage you've caused.	
ROSINELLA:	(*Angry*) That's it. I've had enough. I don't have to stand here and listen to this. You think I'm not suffering? Lucia's more than a niece to me, more than somebody else's lassie that I brought up and grew to love. She's like the child I could never have.	

25

30

35

Silence: BRIDGET thinks, then decides.

MARKS

BRIDGET: The child you never had, eh, Mrs Pedreschi? What about the child I never had?

ROSINELLA: (*Dismissive*) What you going on about now?

BRIDGET: Do you remember that night, I came to see you? I was pregnant.

40   *ROSINELLA shakes her head.*

ROSINELLA: What you saying?

BRIDGET: I was pregnant and it was Franco's baby.

ROSINELLA backs off in disbelief.

Questions

10. Using your own words as far as possible, summarise what happens in the extract. You should make **four** key points.   4

11. Look at lines 11–16.

    Show how both word choice **and** sentence structure are used to reveal Bridget's feelings.   4

12. With reference to **two** examples from the extract show how Rosinella's attitude towards Bridget develops.   4

13. By referring to this extract and to elsewhere in the play, show how the playwright explores family relationships.   8

[Turn over

SECTION 1 — SCOTTISH TEXT — 20 marks

PART B — SCOTTISH TEXT — PROSE

Text 1 — Prose

If you choose this text you may not attempt a question on Prose in Section 2.

Read the extract below and then attempt the following questions.

The Cone-Gatherers by Robin Jenkins

In this extract, Roderick has decided to take some cake to the cone-gatherers, but encounters Duror in the wood.

Peeping through the yew needles, Roderick saw in imagination the door of the hut open, and the cone-gatherers come out, the tall one who slightly limped and always frowned, and the small one who stooped and smiled. Then in the cypress the gun cracked, and the two men lay dead on the grass.

5 It was while he was imagining Duror come stalking out to gloat over the corpses that the idea took root in the boy's mind that perhaps it was Duror himself who was dead. That idea sprouted. Duror had been strolling through the wood, had felt a pain at his heart, and had clutched at the cypress to keep from falling; there he had died, and the green bony arms were propping him up.

10 To Roderick, growing in a time of universal war, distant human death was a commonplace: he had listened to many wireless estimates of enemies killed and had loyally been pleased. Only once, when his grandfather died, had death appeared to him as a tyrant, snatching ruthlessly away what he loved, putting darkness and terror in its place, and at random moments, even in the middle of the night when the rest of the house slept, creating fragments of joy only to

15 annihilate them thereafter. Now the thought of Duror standing dead among the branches of the evergreen brought no hope, but rather began to infect the whole visible world with a sense of loss and desolation and fear. Every single leaf was polluted; even a tiny black beetle close to his head represented the vast tyranny. It was as if all the far off deaths he had rejoiced at were now gathering here around the yew trees to be revenged. Yet was not Duror

20 evil, and if evil died did not goodness triumph? Why then were all the birds not singing, and why did the sun not begin to shine again with morning splendour, and why, above all, was the hut now in shadow? Unable to answer those questions, the boy knelt in an unhappiness too profound and violent for tears or prayer; its only outward signs were paleness and the extra prominence of his teeth.

25 When at last, in the gloaming, Duror moved, it was to the stricken boy like a resurrection, darkening incomprehension and deepening despair. From the arms of the tree Duror stepped forth, and stood for a minute in the clearing in front of the hut. It was a minute of cessation. Incalculable in thought or feeling, gigantic in horror, as if indeed newly come from the dead, Duror merely stood. Then, without any interpretable gesture, and

30 without a sound, he turned and vanished among the trees, as if this time forever.

MARKS

Questions

14. Look at lines 1–9.

    Explain how the writer uses **two** examples of language in these lines to describe what Roderick imagines.

    4

15. Using your own words as far as possible, explain **two** different ways in which Roderick thinks of death in lines 10–19.

    2

16. Explain how the writer uses **two** examples of language to create a frightening atmosphere in lines 17–24.

    4

17. Look at the final sentence of the extract ("Then . . . forever."). By referring to **one** example of word choice, explain how the writer makes Duror's actions appear dramatic.

    2

18. With reference to the extract and to elsewhere in the novel, show how war is an important feature of the novel.

    8

[Turn over

OR

Text 2 — Prose

If you choose this text you may not attempt a question on Prose in Section 2.

Read the extract below and then attempt the following questions.

The Testament of Gideon Mack by James Robertson

The following extract is from the prologue. The editor has just described Gideon Mack's fall into the Black Jaws.

However, three days after this incident, while the community was still coming to terms with its loss, the body of Mr Mack was found washed up on the bank of the Keldo a short distance downstream of the Black Jaws. Not only had the water apparently carried him through its unknown course, but, even more amazingly, he was alive, and without a broken bone in his
5   body. True, he was badly battered, he had a large bruise on the side of his head, and his right leg had sustained some kind of internal damage which left him with a severe limp, but he had somehow survived three nights outdoors and a subterranean journey that no creature, except a fish, could have been expected to survive. He was taken to hospital in Dundee, where he remained unconscious but stable for a day and a half. When he came round he astonished
10 medical staff by making such a speedy recovery that less than a week after the accident he was discharged and sent home.

Back in Monimaskit, Mr Mack convalesced at his manse and seemed in no great hurry to resume his pastoral duties. It was at this time that he began to talk to some people of his experience. He claimed that he had been rescued from the river by a stranger, a man
15 inhabiting the caverns through which he said it passed, and that he had been looked after by this individual. This seemed improbable enough, but Mr Mack went on to assert that this person was none other than the Devil, and that they had had several long conversations in the course of the three days. These remarks were taken by the minister's friends as indication of a severe shock to his system, and possibly of damage to the brain
20 sustained during his ordeal. Others, however, were less concerned with his health than with the injury his words might do to the good name of the Church of Scotland.

A few days later, Mr Mack, despite his seeming physical and mental frailty, insisted on taking the funeral service of an old friend, an inhabitant of Monimaskit, conducting the event in a way which some considered not just unorthodox and irreverent, but
25 incompatible with the role of a Church of Scotland minister. After the interment he publicly repeated his story that he had met and conversed with the Devil. Finally, at the gathering in the church hall which followed, he made declarations of such a scandalous nature that the Monimaskit Kirk Session had no option but to refer the matter to the local Presbytery.

30 The procedures of the Presbyterian court system are complex, but need not long detain us. Presbytery, having heard the evidence, invited Mr Mack to defend himself. He admitted the truth of the allegations made against him, but denied that he had committed any offence. Presbytery decided to suspend him forthwith pending further investigation and consultation with the Church's legal advisers, until such time as Mr Mack
35 could be brought before a committee of Presbytery for trial. A libel was drawn up and served on him, but no date had been set for the case to be heard when Mr Mack's disappearance brought all proceedings to a halt.

MARKS

Questions

19. Using your own words as far as possible, summarise the main events that followed Gideon Mack's accident, as described in this extract. You should make **four** key points in your answer. 4

20. Look at lines 1-11.

    By referring to **two** examples, explain how the writer uses language to suggest that Gideon's story may be untrue. 4

21. Look at lines 12-29.

    Explain how **two** examples of language are used to describe Gideon's character after the accident. 4

22. With reference to this extract and to elsewhere in the novel, show how an important theme is developed. 8

[Turn over

OR

Text 3 — Prose

If you choose this text you may not attempt a question on Prose in Section 2.

Read the extract below and then attempt the following questions.

Kidnapped by Robert Louis Stevenson

In this extract David Balfour has arrived at the house of Shaws where his uncle Ebenezer lives. Ebenezer has asked David to fetch a chest of family papers from the stair-tower.

It was so dark inside, it seemed a body could scarce breathe; but I pushed out with foot and hand, and presently struck the wall with the one, and the lowermost round of the stair with the other. The wall, by the touch, was of fine hewn stone; the steps too, though somewhat steep and narrow, were of polished mason-work, and regular and solid under
5   foot. Minding my uncle's word about the banisters, I kept close to the tower side, and felt my way in the pitch darkness with a beating heart.

The house of Shaws stood some five full storeys high, not counting lofts. Well, as I advanced, it seemed to me the stair grew airier and a thought more lightsome; and I was wondering what might be the cause of this change, when a second blink of the summer lightning came and
10   went. If I did not cry out, it was because fear had me by the throat; and if I did not fall, it was more by Heaven's mercy than my own strength. It was not only that the flash shone in on every side through breaches in the wall, so that I seemed to be clambering aloft upon an open scaffold, but the same passing brightness showed me the steps were of unequal length, and that one of my feet rested that moment within two inches of the well.

15   This was the grand stair! I thought; and with the thought, a gust of a kind of angry courage came into my heart. My uncle had sent me here, certainly to run great risks, perhaps to die. I swore I would settle that 'perhaps', if I should break my neck for it; got me down upon my hands and knees; and as slowly as a snail, feeling before me every inch, and testing the solidity of every stone, I continued to ascend the stair. The darkness, by
20   contrast with the flash, appeared to have redoubled; nor was that all, for my ears were now troubled and my mind confounded by a great stir of bats in the top part of the tower, and the foul beasts, flying downwards, sometimes beat about my face and body.

The tower, I should have said, was square; and in every corner the step was made of a great stone of a different shape, to join the flights. Well, I had come close to one of these
25   turns, when, feeling forward as usual, my hand slipped upon an edge and found nothing but emptiness beyond it. The stair had been carried no higher: to set a stranger mounting it in the darkness was to send him straight to his death; and (although, thanks to the lightning and my own precautions, I was safe enough) the mere thought of the peril in which I might have stood, and the dreadful height I might have fallen from, brought out
30   the sweat upon my body and relaxed my joints.

But I knew what I wanted now, and turned and groped my way down again, with a wonderful anger in my heart. About half-way down, the wind sprang up in a clap and shook the tower, and died again; the rain followed; and before I had reached the ground level it fell in buckets. I put out my head into the storm, and looked along towards the kitchen. The door, which I had shut
35   behind me when I left, now stood open, and shed a little glimmer of light; and I thought I could see a figure standing in the rain, quite still, like a man hearkening. And then there came a blinding flash, which showed me my uncle plainly, just where I had fancied him to stand; and hard upon the heels of it, a great tow-row of thunder.

MARKS

Questions

23. Look at lines 1-6.

    By referring to **two** examples from these lines, explain how the writer creates a sense of fear and/or uncertainty. 4

24. Look at lines 15-16.

    Using your own words as far as possible, explain what David suddenly realises at this point in the extract and how this affects his mood. 2

25. Look at lines 23-38.

    Using your own words as far as possible, summarise the remainder of David's journey.

    You should make **four** key points. 4

26. Look at lines 31-38.

    Explain how any **one** example of the writer's use of language in these lines contributes to the vivid description of the storm. 2

27. With reference to this extract and to elsewhere in the novel, show how the writer uses drama and/or tension to create a powerful adventure story. 8

[Turn over

OR

Text 4 — Prose

If you choose this text you may not attempt a question on Prose in Section 2.

Read the extract below and then attempt the following questions.

The Painter by Iain Crichton Smith

The narrator is describing a fight in the village.

But that was not what I meant to tell since the fight in itself, though unpleasant, was not evil. No, as I stood in the ring with the others, excited and horrified, I saw on the edge of the ring young William with his paint-brush and canvas and easel painting the fight. He was sitting comfortably on a chair which he had taken with him and there was no
5   expression on his face at all but a cold clear intensity which bothered me. It seemed in a strange way as if we were asleep. As the scythes swung to and fro, as the faces of the antagonists became more and more contorted in the fury of battle, as their cheeks were suffused with blood and rage, and their teeth were drawn back in a snarl, he sat there painting the battle, nor at any time did he make any attempt to pull his chair back from
10   the arena where they were engaged.

I cannot explain to you the feelings that seethed through me as I watched him. One feeling was partly admiration that he should be able to concentrate with such intensity that he didn't seem able to notice the danger he was in. The other feeling was one of the most bitter disgust as if I were watching a gaze that had gone beyond the human and which was as
15   indifferent to the outcome as a hawk's might be. You may think I was wrong in what I did next. I deliberately came up behind him and upset the chair so that he fell down head over heels in the middle of a brush-stroke. He turned on me such a gaze of blind fury that I was reminded of a rat which had once leapt at me from a river bank, and he would have struck me but that I pinioned his arms behind his back. I would have beaten him if his mother hadn't
20   come and taken him away, still snarling and weeping tears of rage. In spite of my almost religious fear at that moment, I tore the painting into small pieces and scattered them about the earth. Some people have since said that what I wanted to do was to protect the good name of the village but I must in all honesty say that that was not in my mind when I pushed the chair over. All that was in my mind was fury and disgust that this painter should have
25   watched this fight with such cold concentration that he seemed to think that the fight had been set up for him to paint, much as a house exists or an old wall.

It is true that after this no one would speak to our wonderful painter; we felt in him a presence more disturbing than Red Roderick who did after all recover. So disturbed were we by the incident that we would not even retain the happy paintings he had once
30   painted and which we had bought from him, those of the snow and the harvest, but tore them up and threw them on the dung heap.

MARKS

Questions

28. Look at lines 2-5 ("No, as I stood . . . bothered me").

    By referring to **one** example of the writer's use of language explain how William's reaction to the fight is made clear.

    2

29. Look at lines 6-8 ("As the scythes . . . snarl").

    With reference to **two** examples from these lines explain how the writer uses language to describe the dramatic nature of the fight.

    4

30. Look at lines 11-20 ("I cannot . . . tears of rage").

    Explain, in your own words as far as possible, why the narrator felt "admiration" and/or "bitter disgust" towards William the painter. You should make **four** key points in your answer.

    4

31. Look at lines 27-31.

    Explain, using your own words as far as possible, how the villagers react to William after the fight. You should make **two** key points in your answer.

    2

32. With reference to this extract, and to at least one other story by Iain Crichton Smith, show how the writer creates characters who do not appear to fit in with their surroundings.

    8

[Turn over

OR

Text 5 — Prose

If you choose this text you may not attempt a question on Prose in Section 2.

Read the extract below and then attempt the following questions.

***Dear Santa* by Anne Donovan**

Christmas Eve ah'm sittin on the bed in ma pyjamas wi a pad of blue lined paper and a Biro. The room is daurk but the wee bedside lamp makes a white circle that lights up the page ah'm starin at. It's hard tae find the words.

Dear Santa,

5 *Please could you*

I would like

If its no too much bother

But what is it ah'm tryin tae say? Could you make ma mammy love me? That's no Santa's job, he's there tae gie oot sweeties and toys tae weans wanst a year, so there's nae point
10 in askin him. If there is a Santa. Ah look oot the windae; the sky's dirty grey and ah don't think we'll huv a white Christmas somehow.

The door opens and ma mammy comes in. The hall light's on and her fair hair sticks oot all roon her heid, fuzzy and soft. A cannae see her face.

Are ye no asleep yet? It's nine o'clock.

15 *Ah'm writin ma letter tae Santa.*

Santa doesnae come if yer no sleepin. Look, there's Katie, sound.

She bends ower Katie's bed, where she's lyin wi wan airm stickin oot fae under the covers. Ma mammy lifts the bedclothes ower her, then turns tae me.

Hurry up and finish that letter, Alison. Ah'll pit it in fronty the fire and Santa'll get it
20 *when he comes.*

Ma mammy sits on the bed beside me while ah take a clean bit of paper and write dead slow so it's ma best writin.

Dear Santa,

Please could i have a Barbie doll, and a toy dog. I am a good girl.

25 *Love*

Alison

Ah fold the paper twice, print SANTA on the front, then gie it tae ma mammy. She pits it in her pocket and lifts the covers fur me tae get inside. Ah coorie doon, watchin her hair glowin like a halo against the blackness of the room. Ah love strokin her hair, it's that soft
30 and fuzzy but she cannae be bothered wi that and jerks her heid away, sayin don't, you'll mess it up, just lik she does when ma daddy tries tae touch it. But it's that quiet and still and she's in a good mood so ah lift ma haun and touch her hair, just a wee bit.

MARKS

Mammy, how come you've got fair hair and Katie's got fair hair and mines is broon?

You take efter yer daddy and Katie takes efter me.

35 *Ah wisht ah had fair hair.*

How? There's nothing wrang wi broon hair.

Ah wisht ah had hair lik yours.

Ma mammy smiles and the lines roon her eyes get deeper but she looks at me mair soft like.

40 *Go tae sleep hen, or Santa'll no come.*

She bends ower and kisses me, a dry kiss, barely grazin ma cheek, and before ah have time tae kiss her back she's switched off the bedside light, stood up and moved tae the door.

Night, Alison.

Night, Mammy.

45 She goes oot, nearly closin the door, but leavin a wee crack of light fallin across the bedclothes.

Questions

33. Using your own words as far as possible, summarise what happens in the extract. You should make **four** key points.   4

34. With reference to lines 1–11, explain how **two** examples of Donovan's use of language help the reader to understand how Alison finds the task of writing the letter.   4

35. Look at lines 27–46.

(a) Explain how **one** example of Donovan's language helps the reader understand there is a **positive** aspect to Alison's relationship with her mother.   2

(b) Explain how **one** example of Donovan's language helps the reader understand there is a **negative** aspect to Alison's relationship with her mother.   2

36. Characters in Donovan's stories often face personal difficulties. With reference to the extract and to at least one other story, show how personal difficulties are explored.   8

[Turn over

SECTION 1 — SCOTTISH TEXT — 20 marks

PART C — SCOTTISH TEXT — POETRY

Text 1 — Poetry

If you choose this text you may not attempt a question on Poetry in Section 2.

Read the poem below and then attempt the following questions.

Originally by Carol Ann Duffy

We came from our own country in a red room
which fell through the fields, our mother singing
our father's name to the turn of the wheels.
My brothers cried, one of them bawling, *Home,*
5   *Home*, as the miles rushed back to the city,
the street, the house, the vacant rooms
where we didn't live any more. I stared
at the eyes of a blind toy, holding its paw.

All childhood is an emigration. Some are slow,
10 leaving you standing, resigned, up an avenue
where no one you know stays. Others are sudden.
Your accent wrong. Corners, which seem familiar,
leading to unimagined pebble-dashed estates, big boys
eating worms and shouting words you don't understand.
15 My parents' anxieties stirred like a loose tooth
in my head. *I want our own country*, I said.

But then you forget, or don't recall, or change,
and, seeing your brother swallow a slug, feel only
a skelf of shame. I remember my tongue
20 shedding its skin like a snake, my voice
in the classroom sounding just like the rest. Do I only think
I lost a river, culture, speech, sense of first space
and the right place? Now, *Where do you come from?*
strangers ask. *Originally?* And I hesitate.

MARKS

Questions

37. Look at lines 1-8.

    Explain, using your own words as far as possible, what the poet/persona remembers about the journey. You should make **two** key points.   2

38. By referring to **two** examples of the poet's use of language in lines 9-16, explain fully how the poet makes clear the effect(s) of moving home.   4

39. Look at lines 17-21 ("But then . . . like the rest").

    By referring to **two** examples of the poet's use of language explain fully how the poet suggests acceptance of the move.   4

40. Look at the last four words of the poem ("*Originally*? . . . hesitate").

    Explain how any part of this makes an effective ending to the poem.   2

41. By referring closely to this poem, and to at least one other poem by Duffy, show how the poet uses word choice and/or imagery effectively to convey theme(s).   8

[Turn over

OR

Text 2 — Poetry

If you choose this text you may not attempt a question on Poetry in Section 2.

Read the poem below and then attempt the following questions.

Good Friday **by Edwin Morgan**

Three o'clock. The bus lurches
round into the sun. 'D's this go – '
he flops beside me – 'right along Bath Street?
– Oh tha's, tha's all right, see I've
5   got to get some Easter eggs for the kiddies.
I've had a wee drink, ye understand –
ye'll maybe think it's a – funny day
to be celebrating – well, no, but ye see
I wasny working, and I like to celebrate
10 when I'm no working – I don't say it's right
I'm no saying it's right, ye understand – ye understand?
But anyway tha's the way I look at it –
I'm no boring you, eh? – ye see today,
take today, I don't know what today's in aid of,
15 whether Christ was – crucified or was he –
rose fae the dead like, see what I mean?
You're an educatit man, you can tell me –
– Aye, well. There ye are. It's been seen
time and again, the working man
20 has nae education, he jist canny – jist
hasny got it, know what I mean,
he's jist bliddy ignorant – Christ aye,
bliddy ignorant. Well –' The bus brakes violently,
he lunges for the stair, swings down – off,
25 into the sun for his Easter eggs,
on very
        nearly
            steady
                legs.

MARKS

Questions

42. Look at lines 2-13 ("D's this go . . . boring you, eh?").

By referring to two examples of his speech, explain **two** things we learn about the drunk man.

4

43. Look at lines 14-23.

(a) Comment on the effectiveness of **one** feature of the poet's use of language in creating realistic speech.

2

(b) Show how any **two** examples of the use of word choice makes clear the poem's main ideas or central concerns.

4

44. How effective do you find lines 23-29 as a conclusion to the poem? You should refer to **one** example from these lines and to the ideas and/or language of the rest of the poem.

2

45. By referring closely to this poem and to at least one other poem, show how Morgan explores important human themes.

8

[Turn over

OR

Text 3 — Poetry

If you choose this text you may not attempt a question on Poetry in Section 2.

Read the poem below and then attempt the following questions.

***Sounds of the day* by Norman MacCaig**

When a clatter came,
it was horses crossing the ford.
When the air creaked, it was
a lapwing seeing us off the premises
5   of its private marsh. A snuffling puff
ten yards from the boat was the tide blocking and
unblocking a hole in a rock.
When the black drums rolled, it was water
falling sixty feet into itself.

10   When the door
scraped shut, it was the end
of all the sounds there are.

You left me
beside the quietest fire in the world.

15   I thought I was hurt in my pride only,
forgetting that,
when you plunge your hand in freezing water,
you feel
a bangle of ice round your wrist
20   before the whole hand goes numb.

MARKS

Questions

46. Look at lines 1–9.

Explain fully, in your own words as far as possible, how the poet feels about the "sounds of the day".   2

47. Look again at lines 1–9.

By referring to **one** example of the poet's word choice, explain how the poet suggests that disturbance or upset is to follow.   2

48. Look at lines 10–14.

By referring to **two** examples of the writer's use of language, explain fully how the poet makes it clear that the mood or atmosphere of the poem has now changed.   4

49. Look at lines 15–20.

By referring to **two** examples of word choice or imagery, explain fully how the poet makes clear the effects of his experience.   4

50. By referring to this poem, and to at least one other by MacCaig, show how strong feelings are a feature of his poetry.   8

[Turn over

OR

Text 4 — Poetry

If you choose this text you may not attempt a question on Poetry in Section 2.

Read the poem below and then attempt the following questions.

***Keeping Orchids* by Jackie Kay**

The orchids my mother gave me when we first met
are still alive, twelve days later. Although

some of the buds remain closed as secrets.
Twice since I carried them back, like a baby in a shawl,

5   from her train station to mine, then home. Twice
since then the whole glass carafe has crashed

falling over, unprovoked, soaking my chest of drawers.
All the broken waters. I have rearranged

the upset orchids with troubled hands. Even after
10   that the closed ones did not open out. The skin

shut like an eye in the dark; the closed lid.
Twelve days later, my mother's hands are all I have.

Her face is fading fast. Even her voice rushes
through a tunnel the other way from home.

15   I close my eyes and try to remember exactly:
a paisley pattern scarf, a brooch, a navy coat.

A digital watch her daughter was wearing when she died.
Now they hang their heads,

and suddenly grow old — the proof of meeting. Still,
20   her hands, awkward and hard to hold

fold and unfold a green carrier bag as she tells
the story of her life. Compressed. Airtight.

A sad square, then a crumpled shape. A bag of tricks.
Her secret life — a hidden album, a box of love letters.

25   A door opens and closes. Time is outside waiting.
I catch the draught in my winter room.

Airlocks keep the cold air out.
Boiling water makes flowers live longer. So does

cutting the stems with a sharp knife.

MARKS

Questions

51. Using your own words as far as possible, explain what happens in lines 1–10 of this poem. You should make **two** key points.

2

52. Look again at lines 1–13 ("The orchids . . . fading fast.").

Explain how the poet uses **one** example of word choice and **one** feature of structure to develop the idea of time.

4

53. Look at lines 13–29 ("Even her voice . . . sharp knife.").

By referring to **three** examples of the poet's use of language, explain how the poet creates a sense of awkwardness about the meeting.

6

54. By referring closely to this poem and to at least one other poem by Kay, show how the poet uses personal experience to explore wider themes.

8

[END OF SECTION 1]

[Turn over

SECTION 2 — CRITICAL ESSAY — 20 marks

Attempt ONE question from the following genres — Drama, Prose, Poetry, Film and Television Drama, or Language.

Your answer must be on a different genre from that chosen in Section 1.

You should spend approximately 45 minutes on this Section.

DRAMA

> *Answers to questions in this part should refer to the text and to such relevant features as characterisation, key scene(s), structure, climax, theme, plot, conflict, setting . . .*

1. Choose a play which explores an important relationship, for example, husband and wife, leader and follower, parent and child, or any other relationship.

   Describe this relationship and then, by referring to appropriate techniques, explain how the relationship develops.

2. Choose a play which explores an issue or theme which interests you.

   By referring to appropriate techniques, explain how this issue or theme is explored.

PROSE

> *Answers to questions in this part should refer to the text and to such relevant features as characterisation, setting, language, key incident(s), climax, turning point, plot, structure, narrative technique, theme, ideas, description . . .*

3. Choose a novel **or** short story **or** work of non-fiction which has a key moment.

   Give a brief account of the key moment and, by referring to appropriate techniques, show how it is significant to the text as a whole.

4. Choose a novel **or** short story in which there is an interesting character.

   By referring to appropriate techniques, show how the author makes the character interesting.

POETRY

Answers to questions in this part should refer to the text and to such relevant features as word choice, tone, imagery, structure, content, rhythm, rhyme, theme, sound, ideas . . .

5. Choose a poem which describes a person or a place or an event in a memorable way.

   By referring to poetic techniques, explain how the poet makes this poem so memorable.

6. Choose a poem which deals with a powerful emotion.

   By referring to poetic techniques, show how the poet creates the powerful emotion.

FILM AND TELEVISION DRAMA

Answers to questions in this part should refer to the text and to such relevant features as use of camera, key sequence, characterisation, mise-en-scène, editing, setting, music/sound, special effects, plot, dialogue . . .

7. Choose a scene or sequence from a film or TV drama which shocks or surprises you in some way.

   By referring to appropriate techniques, show how in this scene or sequence the element of surprise is made effective.

8. Choose a film or TV drama in which there is a character about whom you have mixed feelings.

   Show why this character is important to the film or TV drama as a whole and by referring to appropriate techniques, explain how these mixed feelings are created.

* "TV drama" includes a single play, a series or a serial.

[Turn over

LANGUAGE

> *Answers to questions in this part should refer to the text and to such relevant features as register, accent, dialect, slang, jargon, vocabulary, tone, abbreviation . . .*

9. Choose an advertisement which aims to persuade you to buy a product, or to support the aims of a particular group.

   By referring to specific examples from the advertisement, explain how persuasive language is used.

10. Consider the distinctive language used by any group of people from the same place, or with the same job, or the same interest . . .

    By referring to specific examples, explain how the distinctive language of the group is different from the language used by the general population.

[END OF SECTION 2]

[END OF QUESTION PAPER]

NATIONAL 5

Answers

NATIONAL 5 ENGLISH 2014

READING FOR UNDERSTANDING, ANALYSIS AND EVALUATION

1. Candidates should paraphrase "wretchedly indulgent".

   - eg appallingly/dreadfully/extremely/shamefully – ie appreciation of the intensifying function of "wretchedly"
   - eg (over-) tolerant/libertarian/lenient/non-disciplinarian (accept colloquial "soft")
   - 1 mark for reference to "revisiting one's own childhood" (eg comparing one's own childhood).

2. Candidates should identify the structural link, but may do so in either direction

   Selection and identified reference from examples below – no "mix and match"

   or

   Selection identified as looking back

   Selection identified as looking forward

   - "When I was little" looks back to (idea of) "one's own childhood"
   - "given no choices" looks forward to (list of words suggesting) idea of compulsion/(comparative) deprivation
   - "I could only choose what to read" looks forward to "we had all the books we could read".

3. Candidates should draw inferences from the writer's use of language to show appreciation of this important idea

   Word choice

   - "only once" suggests rarity of eating out
   - "motorway café" implies moderately-priced venue
   - "wincing" suggests pained reaction to perceived expense
   - "wincing" or "stomach-churning" suggests repellent nature of comestibles
   - "spag bol" suggests cheap option
   - "From the children's menu" suggests limitation of choice
   - "mainly spent "wooding" for winter fuel" suggests lack of facilities/choice/spartan nature of activity
   - "on rainswept hillsides" suggests spartan nature of activity
   - "(father would invariably book) cheap (overnight ferry crossings)" suggests thrift/parsimony
   - "He would never shell out for a cabin" suggests thrift/parsimony
   - "there was nothing to do for weeks on end except rake leaves" suggests lack of facilities/choice/spartan nature of activity.

Sentence structure

   - (idea of) minor sentence or brevity of "From the children's menu" complements idea of lack of choice/adds emphasis
   - (idea of parenthetical) insertion of "mainly spent "wooding" for winter fuel on rainswept hillsides" illustrates/develops/exemplifies idea of lack of facilities/choice.

4. Candidates should offer a gloss of both words and a correct analytic comment

   - "benign" (eg kind/caring/compassionate/well-meant)
   - "neglect (eg ignoring/leaving alone/not paying attention to, but synonym should not have critical connotation);
   - (idea of) paradox/oxymoron/contrast.

5. Candidates will make selections and offer correct explanations of their effect – these require the drawing of inferences from connotations and/or nuances

   - "manic (mum)" suggests/indicates excess/(near-) insanity
   - "(calls herself a) Tiger Mother" suggests excessive competitiveness/ambition
   - "produce" suggests parenthood being analogous to a manufacturing process
   - Any part of "straight-A ...superkids" suggests excessive ambition
   - "pushy" suggests assertiveness/forcefulness
   - "anxious" suggests over-concern/worry/angst
   - "helicopter parents" or "hover" suggests excessive proximity/involvement
   - "mothers pulled out their sons because the weather forecast was 'rainy'" suggests over-protectiveness/feather-bedding
   - "traumatic" suggests deleterious effect of parental involvement
   - "over-involvement" states excess/inappropriateness of parental attachment
   - "mummies and daddies" allows the inference that (eg) parental view of relationship is inappropriate.

6. Comment may express approval or disapproval.

   Candidates may comment on expression of

   - diversity
   - high achievement
   - preternatural quality
   - hyphenation
   - the effect of a list.

7. Candidates have to select and comment upon aspects of the writer's use of language, to show (inferred) understanding of the father's attitude.

   Apparent attitude:

   - Uses the word "great" **or** an exclamation mark **or** "cried" to suggest enthusiasm.

Actual attitude:

- did not miss a beat" suggests calmness
- "astutely" suggests wisdom
- "if he approved the plan, I would never carry it out" shows (inferable) disapproval.

8. Candidates have to identify two similarities, either by specific reference or expression of more generalised comparisons.

Possible examples include:

- undergoing training/going on courses/taking classes in it
- childcare vouchers
- aims imposed by government/rules
- professional advice/support eg online
- sources of advice
- idea of multiplicity of activities
- idea of diversity of activities
- idea of constantly being on duty
- idea of bureaucratic vigilance.

9. Candidates have to recognise and restate key points.

Any five points from:

Then

Glosses of

- "we were given no choices" eg children were not given options/consulted
- "There was not so much stuff" eg children had fewer possessions
- "we made our own fun" eg children entertained themselves
- "Our parents provided us with the essentials" eg care was basic , parents were not so generous
- "then got on with their own lives" eg parents were more remote/hands-off
- "there was not the expectation of having every wish granted" eg children did not anticipate being given everything they wanted
- "My parents were so hard-up" eg reference to spartan holiday travel and activities
- "Keeping children busy and happy was not a parental priority" eg parents' first concern was not their children's pleasure
- Lack of school "involvement" eg skimpy attention paid to reports, non-attendance at meetings
- "It was the complete opposite in my day" eg lack of involvement pre-tertiary education
- "Becoming a mother or father is no longer something you just are" eg people discovered what to do as they went along.

Now

Glosses of

- "wretchedly indulgent state of modern parenting" eg parents are excessively lenient/lax/soft
- "many of my son's 15-year-old friends have iPods, iPads, MacBooks ... Pay Pal, eBay and iTunes accounts" eg children have many/a variety of modern devices

- "unlimited access to their parents' credit cards" eg children are given a great deal of/excessive financial extravagance
- "I can't repeat this sensible regime ..." eg parents are unable to be as removed as hers were
- "examples of 'wet parenting' abound" eg there are many instances of excessive/over-indulgent/over-protective behaviour
- "(traumatic level of) parental over-involvement just at the exact moment that mummies and daddies are supposed to be letting go" eg parents are too concerned/interfering/hands-on when their children are older
- "Parenting is something you do ... has become subsidised and professionalised" eg parents now are more rule-bound/have more people telling them what to do.

CRITICAL READING

SECTION 1 – Scottish Text

Generic instructions for the 8 marks questions on all texts.

Candidates may choose to answer in **bullet points** in this final question, or write a number of linked statements. There is **no requirement** to write a "mini essay".

Up to 2 marks can be achieved for identifying elements of **commonality** as identified in the question.

A further 2 marks can be gained for **reference to the extract given**.

4 additional marks can be awarded for similar references to **at least one other text/part of the text** by the writer.

<u>In practice this means:</u>

Identification of commonality (e.g.: theme, central relationship, importance of setting, use of imagery, development in characterisation, use of personal experience, sue of narrative style, or any other key element ...)

from the extract:

1 × relevant reference to technique	1 × appropriate comment
OR	
1 × relevant reference to idea	1 × appropriate comment
OR	
1 × relevant reference to feature	1 × appropriate comment
OR	
1 × relevant reference to text	1 × appropriate comment

(maximum of 2 marks only for discussion of extract)

from **at least one other/text part of the text:**

as above (× 2) for **up to 4 marks**

SCOTTISH TEXT — DRAMA

Text 1 — Drama — *Bold Girls* by Rona Munro

1. Candidates should show how the word choice and/or sentence structure create the impression that Marie's daily life is demanding.

   (The volume/range of work she has to do and the general lack of resources is likely to be commented upon.)

   1 mark for selection of relevant quotation about **word choice**.

   1 mark for appropriate comment. 1 mark for selection of relevant reference to **sentence structure**.

   1 mark for appropriate comment.

   Examples of word choice include:

   - use of plural on "irons" and "boards" suggests volume of work
   - "piles" suggests the scale of the work to be undertaken
   - "waiting to be smoothed" (personification) suggests demanding nature of house work
   - Description of toys in different states of repair suggests the never ending cycle of pace of life
   - "swallowed up the year's savings" suggests money is tight
   - "pots and pans and steam…" suggests the multiplicity of the tasks to be done
   - "always hot" suggests the relentlessness of the chores
   - "furniture bald with age" suggests lack of money
   - "gleaming clean" suggests how hard Marie works/ house proud
   - "never deserted" suggests little peace
   - "too stuffed" suggests it is cramped
   - "clutter of housework" suggests she never gets to the end of her work
   - "picture of the virgin" suggests she is religious
   - "blown-up photo" suggests sentimentality.

   Examples of sentence structure include:

   - repeated use of "It's" suggests immediacy of domestic life
   - use of complex sentences suggests the scale of the work she does
   - use of semi-colons for expansion of detail intensifies demanding nature of Marie's remit.

2. Deirdre's words and actions create a bleak mood/ atmosphere. Candidates should demonstrate understanding of this through reference to and comment upon one aspect of the **stage directions** and one aspect of her dialogue.

   1 mark for selection of relevant quotation about stage directions.

   1 mark for appropriate comment.

   1 mark for selection of relevant quotation about **dialogue**.

   1 mark for appropriate comment.

   Examples of stage directions include:

   - "not in this room" suggests she is an outsider (not part of community)

   - "crouching on all fours" suggests she is afraid/or in a hostile environment
   - "darkness" suggests bleakness
   - "only her face is visible" suggests mystery/ concealment
   - "wary" suggests suspicion/danger
   - "black-out" at the end of her speech suggests she is an outsider/builds tension.

   Examples of dialogue include:

   - "sun going down" suggests literally lack of light/ metaphorically lack of hope
   - "sky is grey" suggests bleakness/dullness/lack of interest
   - "hills…green" suggests a contrasting brighter setting
   - "I can't hardly see them…" suggests she is cut off from (more) appealing setting
   - "stones" suggests coldness/harshness
   - repetition of "grey" suggests drabness/hopelessness
   - "Somewhere a bird is singing" suggests her environment lacks natural beauty/suggests she knows there is something better elsewhere.
   - "ice cream van" suggests a nostalgia for the past
   - "helicopter overhead" suggests military action/ urban policing/crime
   - "I hear the ice cream van… and the helicopter overhead" suggests the contrast between daily life and extreme circumstances…

3. (a) Candidates must identify Marie's attitude, eg. she treats him kindly **or** is willing to discipline him.

   Candidates might provide an example of her kindness and an example of discipline.

   Examples of kindness include:

   - asks him about the flavour of the crisps he wanted
   - tells him he can swap them
   - deals with him immediately ("hurls the bag")
   - she explains her decisions to him.

   Examples of discipline include:

   - she restricts the intake of his food
   - she tells him to pick up the crisps
   - she tells him not to be "so bold".

   (b) 1 mark for identification of/comment on Marie's attitude – eg. she accepts that she has a lot of work to do/tries to do all her chores speedily/successfully.

   Candidates should quote and comment on any one aspect of Marie's efficiency.

   1 mark for identification/comment and one mark for relevant quotation.

   or

   Relevant summary of Marie's attitude (without quotation) towards her daily routine – up to 2 marks.

   Examples of Marie's efficiency include:

   - "starts two jobs simultaneously" suggests competence/skill
   - "First…then" suggests a logical approach to her tasks/running order

- "needs ironing and what doesn't" suggests an economy of effort/doesn't do needless jobs
  - "sorts a few items then starts peeling potatoes" suggests the range of tasks to be undertaken
  - "all her movements have a frenetic efficiency" suggests her competence in all respects.

4. Candidates should identify areas of difficulty in the characters' lives from this extract and elsewhere in the play.

   Possible areas for comment are:

   - the setting of the play is bleak and there is the constant threat of violence
   - the women do not have a lot of money and struggle to make ends meet
   - the women do not have a male figure at home to help them with family life
   - the community in which they live is intrusive and there is a lack of privacy
   - the women have committed immoral acts which they hide from others
   - the women have dreams and aspirations beyond what they can secure.

   Candidates may choose to answer in **bullet points** in this final question, or write a number of linked statements. There is **no requirement** to write a 'mini essay'.

   Up to 2 marks can be achieved for identifying elements of **commonality** as identified in the question.

   A further 2 marks can be achieved for **reference to the extract given**.

   4 additional marks can be awarded for similar references to **at least one other part of the text** by the writer.

   <u>In practice this means:</u>

   Identification of commonality (eg: theme, central relationship, importance of setting, use of imagery, development in characterisation, use of personal experience, use of narrative style, or any other key element...)

   from the extract:

   1 × relevant reference to technique

   1 × appropriate comment

   or

   1 × relevant reference to idea

   1 × appropriate comment

   or

   1 × relevant reference to feature

   1 × appropriate comment

   or

   1 × relevant reference to text

   1 × appropriate comment

   (maximum of 2 marks only for discussion of extract)

   from **at least one other part of the text:**

   as above (× 2) for **up to 4 marks**

Text 2 — Drama — *Sailmaker* by Alan Spence

5. Any two key points.

   Candidates are expected to use their own words.

   Possible answers include:

   - Davie comes home drunk

- Alec is worried
- Alec is annoyed
- Alec complains about the state of the house
- Davie tries to defend the way things are
- Alec becomes frustrated that his father will not move on with his life and challenges him
- Davie will not admit his interest in the woman he has met in the pub
- Davie slaps Alec for his rudeness/directness ...
- Alec is left reflecting on the way his relationship with his father has changed/broken down
- Alec is trying to remember something but is unsure what it is.

6. (a) Candidates should identify or comment on an appropriate feeling.

   This feeling should be supported by an appropriate quotation or reference.

   Possible answers include:

   Alec is feeling angry/frustrated/let down ...

   Evidence might include:

   - Alec criticises the untidy/unclean house – "Look at the state ae us"/"livin like bloody Steptoe and Son"/"Place is like a midden"/"When did we last gie it a good clean?"/"Needs gutted"
   - Alec is annoyed that the electricity has been cut off – "Nae light"
   - Alec criticises Davie for going to the pub instead of taking responsibility – "ye go an get bevvied"
   - Alec is frustrated that Davie seems to like women but won't commit to a relationship – "That was no lady, that was a really nice person"
   - Alec's sarcastic tone conveys his frustration – stage direction
   - Alec's question reflects his frustration – "Why don't ye just admit that ye fancy her?".

   (b) Candidates should identify at least two appropriate feelings

   One quotation or reference to language technique (1 mark)

   Appropriate comment about feeling (1 mark)

   Possible answers include:

   Davie is feeling upset/resigned/defensive/fleetingly positive or cheerful/ultimately angry ...

   Evidence might include:

   - defends his lack of cleaning – "It's hard son"/"It's no easy on yer own"
   - defensive with Alec when he mentions going to the pub – "Ye'd think ah came in steamin every night"
   - feels he is entitled to a night out – "Nae harm in it"
   - emphasises that by repeating it in lines 7 and 15

- cheerful when he remembers the evening and the singing – "Wee sing song"/"That lassie's a rare singer"
- angry with Alec at the end (perhaps because Alec's challenge is uncomfortable for him) – stage directions – "slaps him, exits".

7. Alec's state of mind should be justified with reference to an example of word-choice

and

appropriate comment

and

Alec's state of mind should be justified with identification of a feature of sentence structure and appropriate comment

Both word-choice and sentence structure should be justified for full marks.

Possible answers include:

Alec is confused/regretful

Word-choice:

- repetition of "somethin"/"something" vagueness suggest he is confused/seeking answers
- "sometimes" again suggests lack of pattern in his life /confusion
- "lost"/"looking for" suggests he is confused /seeking answers …
- language is mostly English – he has moved on/ changed and doesn't understand this/thinks he no longer belongs …

Sentence Structure:

- three questions suggests he is looking for answers
- use of ellipsis struggling to find the words to finish the sentence
- short/abrupt sentence – "God knows" suggests he cannot work out what has gone wrong
- series of short sentences/questions thoughts are not flowing well/confused ideas.

8. Candidates should identify the way in which Alec has changed with reference to this extract and to elsewhere in the play.

Both sides of the change (eg. working class to middle class/using Scots to English/school to university) should be identified for 1 mark.

Supporting evidence /comment for each side can be rewarded with 1 mark each.

- Alec has become more (openly) critical of his father/ has lost respect for him.
- he becomes increasingly more responsible and mature
- Alec becomes more distant from his father and more of a contrast to him
- ultimately, the roles reverse and Alec becomes more like the father in the relationship
- however, Alec still feels something is missing in his life.

Extract: Alec is critical of his father

Elsewhere:
At start of play Alec shows a lot of respect and admiration for his father especially in his conversations with Ian in Act 1 where he boasts of his dad's sailmaking skills and shows off his dad's tools. He also has faith in his father that he will fix the yacht that he also shows to Ian.

Extract: Alec criticises his father's drinking

Elsewhere:

Earlier in Act 1 Alec says to Davie 'You've been drinkin. I can smell it.' But that is all he says – he simply makes a statement; he does not criticise or antagonise Davie further about it.

Extract: relationship is at its lowest point as Alec is very critical and Davie ends up slapping him

Elsewhere:
Earlier in Act 2 – Alec criticises his dad's cooking so there are signs of this side of Alec before now

End of play – Alec finally questions Davie about why he gambles which he always just accepted before

End of play – Alec tells Davie he plans to move out

Prior to this event in the extract, Alec tells of a time Davie teased him about a girl to the extent Alec was so angry he hit his father; the complete opposite of what has happened here highlighting the role reversal

Extract: it is Alec who criticises the state of the house

Elsewhere:
Twice in Act 1 – at start and later on – it is Davie who comments on the state of the house – not Alec and Alec never responds showing he had no interest/this wasn't his concern before

Alec also shows his maturity and sense of responsibility when he offers Davie the money for the electricity bill.

It is also Alec who suggests burning the furniture at the end of the play to keep warm, showing his ability to present solutions to problems

Extract: Alec still questions what he has lost, what is missing from his life

Elsewhere:
Earlier, Alec has similar thoughts after the argument with Davie about his cooking

Also, earlier in the play, Alec turns to religion to try to fill a gap in his life and has doubts about his reasons for his interest in the church

Candidates may choose to answer in **bullet points** in this final question, or write a number of linked statements. There is **no requirement** to write a 'mini essay'.

Up to 2 marks can be achieved for identifying elements of **commonality** as identified in the question.

A further 2 marks can be achieved for **reference to the extract given**.

4 additional marks can be awarded for similar references to **at least one other part of the text** by the writer.

In practice this means:

Identification of commonality (eg: theme, central relationship, importance of setting, use of imagery, development in characterisation, use of personal experience, use of narrative style, or any other key element…)

from the extract:

1 × relevant reference to technique

1 × appropriate comment

or

1 × relevant reference to idea

1 × appropriate comment

or

1 × relevant reference to feature

1 × appropriate comment

or

1 × relevant reference to text

1 × appropriate comment

(maximum of 2 marks only for discussion of extract)

from **at least one other part of the text**:

as above (× 2) for **up to 4 marks**

Text 3 – Drama – *Tally's Blood* by Ann Marie de Mambro

9. (a) Candidates should identify two stereotypes then explain how they are shown to be false.

    - Rosinella says Italian men are willing to work hard/no one works as hard as them

    - but Hughie is shown to be working hard/Hughie is described as "working like a trojan"

    - Rosinella says that "Nobody loves their families like the Italians"

    - but Hughie is shown to love his mum by going home to sit with her **or** Bridget is willing to help her brother out with his wedding preparations because his mum can't

    - Rosinella criticises Hughie's brother (and in effect all Scottish men) for drinking

    - but then Massimo reaches for the wine **or** Hughie refuses a drink.

    (b) Identification of reaction (1 mark)

    Explanation/justification (1 mark)

    - think it is funny

    - think it is ironic

    - think Rosinella is stupid/prejudiced for saying it

    - they might be angry

    - any other appropriate audience reaction accepted with explanation.

10. (a) Identify two examples of Rosinella's kindness/caring

    - offers Hughie food

    - knows Rigatoni is Hughie's favourite

    - gives Hughie money for a present for his brother

    - is interested in/asks about Hughie's family

    - calls Hughie "son".

    (b) Identify two examples of Rosinella's unkindness/unpleasantness.

    - suggests Hughie's brother has got his fiancée pregnant

    - assumes Bridget is going out to see a man but calls it 'winching' to cheapen it

    - Lucia is too scared to ask her something (to go to the wedding)

    - suggests that Bridget will never get married

    - suggests that Hughie's brother will be out drinking days after his wedding

    - doesn't realise that neither Massimo or Lucia are interested in her conversation

    - keeps insisting that she is 'right' in the things she is saying

    - Rosinella makes prejudiced statements.

11. Candidates are asked to identify two examples:

'wee bit'/'up the road'/'winching'/'up to it'/'am n't'/'poke'/'wee'/'pals'/'son'/'mammy'/'give's a hand'/'Hang on a minute'/'Help them out'/'shooshes'

12. Candidates should discuss how racism is explored in this extract and elsewhere in the play.

    Possible answers may include:

    - Rosinella's comments from elsewhere about Italians (always positive) eg makes you special, makes you more attractive, etc

    - Rosinella's comments from elsewhere about Scots (usually negative) eg can't look after their children properly, allow their girls to go out unsupervised, have looser moral standards, etc

    - Rosinella's racism towards Bridget when she is dating Franco

    - Rosinella's racism towards Hughie when he is in love with Lucia

    - the treatment of Massimo by the public at the outbreak of war/when his shop is attacked

    - the treatment of the Italian people who were taken during the war

    - Rosinella's refusal to let go of what happened to them during the war

    - Lucia's mimicry of the school teacher showing the racism she has suffered

    - there may be valid comments about the war itself as an example of Nationalism becoming racism.

    Candidates may choose to answer in **bullet points** in this final question, or write a number of linked statements. There is **no requirement** to write a 'mini essay'.

    Up to 2 marks can be achieved for identifying elements of **commonality** as identified in the question.

    A further 2 marks can be achieved for **reference to the extract given**.

    4 additional marks can be awarded for similar references to **at least one other part of the text** by the writer.

    <u>In practice this means:</u>

    Identification of commonality (eg: theme, central relationship, importance of setting, use of imagery, development in characterisation, use of personal experience, use of narrative style, or any other key element…)

    from the extract:

    1 × relevant reference to technique

    1 × appropriate comment

    or

    1 × relevant reference to idea

    1 × appropriate comment

    or

    1 × relevant reference to feature

    1 × appropriate comment

    or

    1 × relevant reference to text

    1 × appropriate comment

    (maximum of 2 marks only for discussion of extract)

    from **at least one other part of the text**:

    as above (× 2) for **up to 4 marks**

SCOTTISH TEXT – PROSE

Text 1 – Prose – *The Cone-Gatherers* by Robin Jenkins

13. Both emotions for full marks.
    - at first delight/happiness
    - then fear for the animals

14. Can have either aspect for full marks or implied recognition of contrast.

    "marvellous grace and agility" plus comment

    or

    "flew for the doom ahead" plus comment

    or

    Accept grace/doom. Accept a gloss on: they were very beautiful, but they were going to be killed anyway.

15. *Any two from:*
    - "Moaning"
    - "gasping"
    - "Impulse"
    - "Not … so swift and sure of foot"
    - "He fell and rose again"
    - "avoided one tree (only to collide with another close to it)".

16. Two quotations with references and associated comments:
    - "Wails of lament" distress being loudly expressed
    - "Dashed on at demented speed" dashed suggests speed of his movement; demented as though he is mad
    - "A deer screaming" suggests the terror of the animal
    - "Scrabbling around on its hindquarters" the struggle of the wounded animal to escape
    - "Calum saw no one else" unheeding of anything but the animal
    - "Screaming in sympathy" loud distress shared by Calum
    - "Terrified more than ever" implies losing control through fear
    - "It dragged him about with it" creature in its agony instinctively trying to escape, even with Calum holding it.
    - "In mortal agony" unaware of anything but its death throes.
    - "heedless of the danger of being shot" emphasising that he is in such a panic that his personal safety is not important to him.

17. We would expect him to be angry but instead he seems to be enjoying what he is seeing.

    or

    The others are horrified but he is laughing.

    or

    He has planned this so is pleased.

18. Candidates should discuss the portrayal of Duror in this extract and elsewhere in the novel.

    This passage is a culmination of Duror's plot to get rid of the cone gathering brothers, Callum and Neil. The passage holds a great deal of information but we will focus on the parts specifically pertaining to Duror.

    Throughout the novel there is an irrational animosity towards Callum and Neil, but mainly Callum displayed by the gamekeeper, Duror and this passage is the watershed which signals his descent into madness.

    His intention had been to use the deer hunt as a means to cause Callum harm or distress resulting in a more overt obsession.

    He has an obsessive hatred for Callum because he has detested anything misshapen since his younger days and this has manifested itself in his disgust of his bedridden wife whom he cannot even touch.

    He is embittered because of the situation he finds himself in including his relationships with his mother in law, his repeated rejection by the army as this is set during the war and his sense of frustration towards his employer Lady Runcie-Campbell whom he desires but it is a one sided desire.

    L5 **Duror caught sight of them and rushed in pursuit** this is a literal pursuit in the extract but is also the pursuit of his goal to get rid of the brothers throughout the novel, an irrational pursuit.

    L17 **The dogs barked fiercely** and **Duror fired his gun** the word choice of barked fiercely and fired contrasts with words to describe Callum in this extract such as **silent** and **desperate**.

    L22 **Duror bawled to his dogs** a line filled with hard sounding consonants and plosives

    By his would be attack on the brother, it is as if he is simultaneously acting unnaturally and attacking nature itself. This is evident through the word choice of **screaming** to describe the noise made by both Callum and the deer.

    Not only is Callum associated with animal symbolism, Duror himself latterly in the novel can be seen as embodying evil and darkness and in this rural setting can be seen to represent the serpent from the Garden of Eden. It is paradoxical in that his role within the novel is as a gamekeeper on a large estate who should maintain control of the animals.

    At the end of this extract, Duror **came leaping out of the wood** and **seemed to be laughing in some kind of berserk joy**. This overt display of madness contrasts with the reactions of the other witnesses to this event, Captain Forgan, Young Roderick and Lady Runcie-Campbell who are standing **petrified**.

    His abnormal reaction foreshadows his descent into madness and irrational behaviour which leads ultimately to the tragic ending, the murder of Callum and his own suicide.

    Candidates may choose to answer in **bullet points** in this final question, or write a number of linked statements. There is **no requirement** to write a 'mini essay'.

    Up to 2 marks can be achieved for identifying elements of **commonality** as identified in the question.

    A further 2 marks can be achieved for **reference to the extract given**.

    4 additional marks can be awarded for similar references to **at least one other part of the text** by the writer.

    In practice this means:

    Identification of commonality (eg: theme, central relationship, importance of setting, use of imagery, development in characterisation, use of personal experience, use of narrative style, or any other key element...)

from the extract:

1 × relevant reference to technique

1 × appropriate comment

or

1 × relevant reference to idea

1 × appropriate comment

or

1 × relevant reference to feature

1 × appropriate comment

or

1 × relevant reference to text

1 × appropriate comment

(maximum of 2 marks only for discussion of extract)

from **at least one other part of the text:**

as above (× 2) for **up to 4 marks**

Text 2 – Prose – *The Testament of Gideon Mack* by James Robertson

19. Full marks can be obtained in a variety of ways – by making four brief points or by making fewer, more developed points for multiple marks, adding up to 4.

    Possible answers include:

    - freedom ('took me out of myself'/'minister off the leash') with supplementary points about forgetting about job and wider world problems

    - released energy inside him , perhaps with explanation of the candidate's understanding of what that means

    - rebellion against his disapproving parishioners

    - vanity, as he thinks he looks good or runs well

    - loses himself in it to the point that he notices the different sounds his trainers make on different surfaces

    - increased awareness and appreciation of surroundings

    - sense of living life to the full.

20. 1 mark for attitude and 1 mark for appropriate evidence

    Attitude identified is likely to be negative eg not committed, even interested/sees it as a burden/sees himself as a hypocrite etc.

    Plus appropriate evidence.

21. (a) Example (1 mark)

    NB 1 mark for each example given

    or

    One well developed explanation could gain all 3 marks at once.

    Possible answers include:

    - **extended sentence** in first paragraph **giving** all the alternative reasons for running

    - using the **repetition** of 'not'/**parenthesis** adding weight to each point

    - **simple sentence** to emphasise his real reason for running

    - the word 'but' indicates a change in direction

    - **italics** for emphasis of the word 'needed'

    - **repetition** (of the sentence starter 'I ran') to emphasise how much/how freely he ran

    - **use of semicolons** to separate the things he can ignore when running to emphasise the freedom from worry.

    (b) Identification of image (1 mark)

    Brief comment on image (1 mark)

    Relation of image to running (1 mark)

    Possible answers include:

    - 'as if the fire blazing away in there was my fuel' suggests that the energy/heat he refers to is what is propelling him when he runs just as petrol/fuel propels a car/machinery /feels he has to run/is able to run because of this energy.

    - 'emptied my head of work, the Kirk, the world' suggests that running is removing his worries from his head Mack feels free when running.

    - 'difficult issues and awkward individuals were' suggests the issues and people were pushed back which removes his worries /allows him to feel free when he is running.

    - 'their ghosts faded into the trees' suggests his problems disappeared from his mind when running. Mack feels free and relaxed when running.

22. Candidates should discuss one aspect of Gideon Mack's character with reference to this extract and elsewhere in the novel.

    Possible answers may include:

    Need to escape
    Extract: *When I set off...I could feel the disapproval of some of my parishioners*
    Elsewhere in novel: mountains/B and B...

    Reluctance to conform
    Extract: *there was something just no richt about a minister in shorts*
    Elsewhere in novel: references could include wanting to be a school teacher not a minister; funeral for Catherine Craigie; didn't believe in God; Having sex on his marital bed with Elsie...

    Hypocrite
    Extract: *an escapee from my professional hypocrisy, a minister off the leash*
    Elsewhere in novel: *Although within I had abandoned my faith, I still attended church and remained the dutiful son of the manse*; Gideon joins the Church as a minister despite his lack of belief...

    Outsider
    Extract: *The loneliness of the long distance runner*; references to film.
    Elsewhere in novel: References could include when he met the boys in his new school in the 1970s; dual existence – pretending to be one person to satisfy his parents while being someone else to satisfy classmates.

    Represses memories/feelings
    Extract: *Running emptied my head of work, the Kirk, the world*
    Elsewhere in novel: references to hiding feelings; Elsie says "terrible childhood which strangled love at every turn"...

    Frustrated by others
    Extract: *Difficult issues and awkward individuals were repelled by the force of my energy...*

Elsewhere in novel: References to relationship with father; Peter Macmurray and his dislike of Gideon.

Candidates may choose to answer in **bullet points** in this final question, or write a number of linked statements. There is **no requirement** to write a 'mini essay'.

Up to 2 marks can be achieved for identifying elements of **commonality** as identified in the question.

A further 2 marks can be achieved for **reference to the extract given**.

4 additional marks can be awarded for similar references to **at least one other part of the text** by the writer.

<u>In practice this means:</u>

Identification of commonality (eg: theme, central relationship, importance of setting, use of imagery, development in characterisation, use of personal experience, use of narrative style, or any other key element…)

from the extract:

1 × relevant reference to technique

1 × appropriate comment

or

1 × relevant reference to idea

1 × appropriate comment

or

1 × relevant reference to feature

1 × appropriate comment

or

1 × relevant reference to text

1 × appropriate comment

(maximum of 2 marks only for discussion of extract)

from **at least one other part of the text:**

as above (× 2) for **up to 4 marks**

Text 3 — Prose — *Kidnapped* by Robert Lewis Stevenson

23. Four points to be made.

1 mark for each point.

Possible answers include:

- it is foggy
- Alan's boat is struck by the *Covenant*
- Alan's boat is split in half
- Alan's boat sinks
- the whole crew die except Alan
- Alan grabs hold of the *Covenant*'s bowspirit
- Alan is saved and brought on to the *Covenant*.

24. 1 mark for each individual point about his physical appearance and his character.

Candidates must deal with both physical appearance and character for full marks but not necessarily in equal proportion.

Possible answers include:

A gloss of **physical characteristics**:

- "smallish in stature"
- "well set"
- "nimble as a goat"
- "open expression"
- "sunburnt very dark"

- "heavily freckled"
- "pitted with the small-pox"
- "eyes were unusually light"
- (eyes had) "dancing madness"

A gloss on his **character**:

- "His manners … were elegant"
- "he pledged the captain handsomely"
- "engaging"
- "alarming"
- "rather call my friend than my enemy".

25. Candidates should show an awareness of the friction between Alan and Hoseason.

Full marks for two examples with detailed comments.

Possible answers include:

Word choice:

- "still (watching him)" emphasis of the fact that Hoseason has possibly been wary of Alan
- "(still) watching (him)" watching with connotations of careful inspection emphasising possible concern
- "Oho!" exclamatory interjection of surprise and realisation indicates friction in this context
- "(laid his hand) quickly" emphasises the suddenness of Alan's response in reaching for his pistols/ emphasises Alan's concern for his situation/action could also be seen as a response to a slight by Hoseason.
- "(Don't be) hasty" emphasises Hoseason's attempt to quell Alan, or shows his concern about what Alan may do with the pistols.

Metaphor:

- "is that how the wind sets?" emphasises Alan's perception of Hoseason's now clear antagonistic attitude towards him.

Sentence structure:

- "Oho!" exclamatory nature of the interjection
- Rhetorical question – "…is that how the wind sets?" emphasis on the fact that Alan feels he knows Hoseason's antagonistic view of him.
- Repetition of "Don't be …" emphasises Hoseason's attempt to quell Alan, or shows his concern about what Alan may do with the pistols.

26. Candidates should discuss the development of David and Alan's relationship with reference to this extract and to elsewhere in the novel.

Possible references:

The idea of 'commonality' is one which may be established in several ways. It could be made explicit in the candidate response or it could be implicitly delivered through the overall answer of the candidate for this question.

Some possible aspects of the developing relationship between David and Alan which candidates may discuss are:

- the contradictory/contrasting natures of the characters as developed throughout the text;
- tensions in the relationship as it develops throughout the text;
- the theme of duality established by looking at the relationship throughout the text;

- the admiration the characters have for each other at points throughout the texts;
- the developing movement from uncertainty towards true friendship and understanding which is developed throughout the text;
- a mixture of elements from some or all of the above.

The points above could be seen as the more accepted ideas about the relationship between David and Alan in this text. Be open to accepting well-argued points which are not included within the points above.

Candidates may choose to answer in **bullet points** in this final question, or write a number of linked statements. There is **no requirement** to write a 'mini essay'.

Up to 2 marks can be achieved for identifying elements of **commonality** as identified in the question.

A further 2 marks can be achieved f**or reference to the extract given.**

4 additional marks can be awarded for similar references to **at least one other part of the text** by the writer.

<u>In practice this means:</u>

Identification of commonality (eg: theme, central relationship, importance of setting, use of imagery, development in characterisation, use of personal experience, use of narrative style, or any other key element…)

from the extract:

1 × relevant reference to technique

1 × appropriate comment

or

1 × relevant reference to idea

1 × appropriate comment

or

1 × relevant reference to feature

1 × appropriate comment

or

1 × relevant reference to text

1 × appropriate comment

(maximum of 2 marks only for discussion of extract)

from **at least one other part of the text:**

as above (× 2) for **up to 4 marks**

Text 4 – Prose – *The Telegram* by Iain Crichton Smith

27. Example/reference to language feature with comment

Suggested examples include:

Short sentences build up the pace

Sentence structure: sentence beginning 'She had dreamt…' climactic effect

Repetitive sentence structure/'She had dreamt'; 'She could see'; 'She could never..' emphasis on the rising panic of the fat woman

Word choice: we are shown fat woman's thoughts 'Oh pray God…' etc helps us to understand her rising fear/tension/panic

Repetition of 'God'/repeated references to religion like she is praying/becoming hysterical

28. (a) Example with comment

Possible examples/explanations:

- 'lips…white and bloodless' emphasises her state of shock
- 'dreaded' emphasises the worry/panic she feels that her son may be dead.

(b) Example with comment

Possible examples/explanations:

- 'lips pressed closely together' emphasises her attempt to hold back her emotion/expression
- 'wasn't crying or shaking' not showing her emotions
- 'firm voice' does not shake with emotion.

29. Candidates should give four relevant points for 4 marks.

Must be an attempt to use own words.

Suggested answers include:

- she is poor
- struggles to feed herself and her son
- she is a widow/no husband to support her/single parent
- gloss of 'bringing up a son in a village not her own' eg an outsider
- people have been unkind/unsupportive.

30. Candidates should discuss how the writer creates sympathy for a character/characters in this story and in at least one other story by Iain Crichton Smith.

Possible references:

"Mother And Son"
John, central character – Aggression of mother (may be expressed by reference to speech, "she snapped pettishly"); sustained denigration; low self-esteem (because of being butt of others' humour); joblessness; word choice such as his life being "hell", his "loneliness" …

"The Red Door"
Murdo, central character – His unmarried status (reluctance to enter/fear of entering a relationship); his fear of breaching convention despite desire to expand horizons; lack of academic success and clumsiness at school; he has "never been [himself]"; loneliness; unhappiness at lifestyle (repetition of "he didn't like"); the difference of the red door symbolising everything that he was not

"The Painter"
William Murray, focus of account – Ill health; incongruity of this character in a conventional, inward-looking village; the fact that the painting was destroyed by the narrator; ostracisation and banishment of painter

"The Crater"
Lt Robert Mackinnon, central character – Context of war; danger of raid, hazards of No Man's Land; responsibilities of leadership; expression of fear (emphasised by repetition); the awful appearance of the victim in the crater (eg emphasis on colour green); implication of stress shown by (unusual) swearing; irony of victim dying

"In Church"
Lt Colin Macleod, central character – General context of war; specific perception that fate is indifferent to him and his comrades; discomfiting character of (lunatic) "priest"; ending where (defenceless) central character is murdered

Candidates may choose to answer in **bullet points** in this final question, or write a number of linked statements.

There is **no requirement** to write a 'mini essay'.

Up to 2 marks can be achieved for identifying elements of **commonality** as identified in the question.

A further 2 marks can be achieved for **reference to the extract given.**

4 additional marks can be awarded for similar references to **at least one other short story** by the writer.

In practice this means:

Identification of commonality (eg: theme, central relationship, importance of setting, use of imagery, development in characterisation, use of personal experience, use of narrative style, or any other key element...)

from the extract:

1 × relevant reference to technique

1 × appropriate comment

or

1 × relevant reference to idea

1 × appropriate comment

or

1 × relevant reference to feature

1 × appropriate comment

or

1 × relevant reference to text

1 × appropriate comment

(maximum of 2 marks only for discussion of extract)

from **at least one other short story by the writer:**

as above (× 2) for **up to 4 marks**

Text 5 – Prose – *Away in a Manger* **by Anne Donovan**

31. Candidates should make two clear points

    Must make an attempt to use own words.

    - the family go to see the nativity
    - in George Square
    - the mother explains the scene
    - a homeless man has climbed inside the crib to escape the cold
    - they think he is an angel.

32. Identification or exemplification of technique with comment

    Possible answers could include:

    - **Personification**/'staunin' suggests bronze statues are brought to life/which makes them seem more like ordinary human beings.
    - **Metaphor**/the straw is described as a carpet as something familiar (we would see in the home).
    - **Simile**/'what looked like a hoose made of glass'. The manger/crib is surrounded by a glass screen. This is compared again to the ordinary or familiar, the 'hoose' again making it seem less unusual.

    Candidate may refer to Amy from lines 11–29.

    Possible answers could include:

    - questions show that she does not know who they are

- use of dash in line 12 or 14 indicates pause for recognition
- italics (in line 15) for emphasis
- statements followed by question
- exclamation marks (in line 29) for emotion/recognition.

33. Identification of language feature (1 mark)

    Comment on its effect (1 mark)

    - Omission of capital letters/full stops creates the impression of changes of mind.
    - Use of commas (creates pauses), giving us the impression of an idea being challenged/altered/thought through.
    - Sentence structures suggest/sound like someone speaking (out loud).
    - Opening statement 'Sandra wisnae very religious' is then qualified with, 'no religious at all,' then a second time in, 'really'. The final part of the sentence then acts as explanation (that, despite her lack of religious conviction, 'it was nice for wee ones tae have a crib').
    - Parenthesis (line 7) – indication of thinking.

34. Two identifications of word choice with comment on effect

    Possible examples of word choice include:

    - "Huddled" cold/insecure/protecting himself
    - "Hidden" doesn't want to be seen/hiding
    - "a man" no idea of age
    - "Slightly built" unhealthy/underfed
    - "Auld jeans" poverty/lack of money
    - "Thin jaicket" not suited to winter, therefore he is poor/unemployed
    - "Worn trainin shoe" poor/doesn't have a lot of money
    - "Cheapest kind" poverty
    - "Quite young" engages our sympathy/surprise
    - "Pointed face" thin/undernourished
    - "Longish dark hair" uncut as he can't afford it/reminds us of Jesus
    - "Stubbly growth covered his chin" reminds us of Jesus.
    - "Sound asleep" exhausted/tired/engages our sympathy.

35. Candidates should discuss any one theme explored in this story and in at least one other story by Donovan.

    Possible references to theme:

    "Away in a Manger"
    Family relationships, childhood, naiveté, parent/child relationships, misunderstanding, love, generational differences, growing up, Christmas

    "All that Glisters"
    Family relationships, childhood, naiveté, parent/child relationships, misunderstanding, love, generational differences, growing up

    "Dear Santa"
    Family relationships, childhood, parent/child relationships, misunderstanding, love, growing up, Christmas

"Virtual Pals"
Childhood, naiveté, misunderstanding, growing up, love, relationships

"A Chitterin Bite"
Childhood, growing up, relationships, love

"Zimmerobics"
Relationships, generational differences

Candidates may choose to answer in **bullet points** in this final question, or write a number of linked statements. There is **no requirement** to write a 'mini essay'.

Up to 2 marks can be achieved for identifying elements of **commonality** as identified in the question.

A further 2 marks can be achieved for **reference to the extract given**.

4 additional marks can be awarded for similar references to **at least one other short story** by the writer.

In practice this means:

Identification of commonality (eg: theme, central relationship, importance of setting, use of imagery, development in characterisation, use of personal experience, use of narrative style, or any other key element…)

from the extract:

1 × relevant reference to technique

1 × appropriate comment

or

1 × relevant reference to idea

1 × appropriate comment

or

1 × relevant reference to feature

1 × appropriate comment

or

1 × relevant reference to text

1 × appropriate comment

(maximum of 2 marks only for discussion of extract)

from **at least one other short story by the writer:**

as above (× 2) for **up to 4 marks**

SCOTTISH TEXT – POETRY

Text 1 – Poetry – *War Photographs* by Carol Ann Duffy

36. 2 marks can be awarded for two main ideas or concerns shown in stanza one.

    The war photographer:

    - has from become isolated from other people/needs to be alone
    - has been exposed to the pain and suffering of others
    - is very methodical
    - feels he has a duty to inform the public about the pain he has witnessed
    - has travelled to many war zones (needs more than just he is well travelled)
    - has developed a pessimistic world view.

37. 4 marks can be awarded for two examples of language helping to bring out his attitude.

    Example (1 mark) plus comment (1 mark) – any two will gain 4 marks.

Other examples from stanza are acceptable.

- the position of the short emphatic sentence "He has a job to do"
- suggests the photographer's professionalism/matter of fact view of his work.

or

- the need to adopt this attitude as a coping strategy given the horror of his work.
- the word choice of "… did not tremble then" suggests his need to control/suppress his feelings/focused on his job while in the war zone
- the contrast in "though seem to now" suggests the long term emotional effect of what he witnessed abroad/having an impact on him now
- the word choice of "explode"/"nightmare heat" suggests the threat/danger
- the contrast of "Rural England" and "explode"/"nightmare heat" highlights the danger he became accustomed to in the war zone.

or

- the difficulty of re-adjusting to home
- "ordinary pain" suggests his awareness of how trivial the problems faced by people in Britain are (compared to those in the war zones)
- the word choice of "dispel" suggests how shallow/easily addressed he feels the problems faced by people in Britain are.

38. 2 marks can be awarded for one example of dramatic language.

    Example (1 mark) plus comment (1 mark)

    - the positioning of the abrupt sentence "Something is happening" suggests sudden activity
    - the word choice of "twist" suggests violent activity/distorted in pain
    - the ambiguity of "twist before his eyes" suggests the image being revealed but also the distressing nature of the image
    - the word choice of "half formed ghost" suggests being haunted by memories/idea of memories being slowly revealed
    - the word choice of "cries" suggests the anguish of the man's wife
    - the use of sense words such as "blood stained"/"cries" suggests the vivacity of the memory.

39. Candidates should show an understanding of how the content of the last stanza continues ideas and/or language from the first three stanzas.

    - "A hundred agonies" refers to scenes of pain and suffering mentioned earlier
    - the word choice of "black and white" continues the references to the development of photographs/suggests a truthful representation of the suffering
    - the contrast in numbers – "hundred" with "five or six" continues the process of trivialising suffering/callousness to suffering in the war zones
    - the word choice of "prick with tears" is another example of the limited emotional response to the suffering in the war zone

- the juxtaposition/alliteration of "between the bath and the pre-lunch beers" suggests the brief period of concern for the suffering/suggests a contrast between the safety and comfort of life in Britain and the dangers of life in the war zone
- the word choice of "impassively" suggests the beginning of his coping strategy as he flies out to his next assignment
- the word choice of "earns his living" suggests a return of the matter of fact way of viewing his job/ beginning of his coping strategy as he returns to the war zone
- "they do not care" emphasises the indifference of people in Britain to the suffering in the war zones.

40. Candidates should show awareness of the presentation of a main character through ideas and/or language in this poem and at least one other poem by Duffy.

Candidates may refer to how the war photographer has endured an upsetting/difficult experience that has profoundly affected his view of society. This is a theme which emerges in **"Havisham"** and **"Mrs. Midas"** in which the main character has also endured such an experience.

In **"Valentine"**, the speaker is the main character. The speaker gives an account of the experience of sharing valentine's gifts.

In **"Anne Hathaway"**, the speaker is the main character. Here, she reflects on her life with her husband following his death.

In **"Originally"**, the speaker is the main character. Here she reflects on the difficulties she endured when moving from one place to another.

Candidates may choose to answer in **bullet points** in this final question, or write a number of linked statements. There is **no requirement** to write a 'mini essay'.

Up to 2 marks can be achieved for identifying elements of **commonality** as identified in the question.

A further 2 marks can be achieved for **reference to the extract given**.

4 additional marks can be awarded for similar references to **at least one other poem** by the writer.

In practice this means:

Identification of commonality (eg: theme, central relationship, importance of setting, use of imagery, development in characterisation, use of personal experience, use of narrative style, or any other key element...)

from the extract:

1 × relevant reference to technique

1 × appropriate comment

or

1 × relevant reference to idea

1 × appropriate comment

or

1 × relevant reference to feature

1 × appropriate comment

or

1 × relevant reference to text

1 × appropriate comment

(maximum of 2 marks only for discussion of extract)

from **at least one poem** by the writer:

as above (× 2) for **up to 4 marks**

Text 2 – Poetry – *In the Snack-bar* by Edwin Morgan

41. (a) Candidates should identify two of the poem's main ideas or central concerns that are introduced in this extract.

Possible answers:

- how the less fortunate are treated in society
- appearance and reality
- isolation/loneliness
- society's selfishness/lack of interest in helping others
- for some disabled people tasks that might seem to be straightforward to us can involve many potential hazards
- public places can be full of difficulties for some disabled people
- society fears what looks strange
- some disabled people have no choice but to rely on strangers to help them.

(b) Examples of use of language with comment on how it clarifies a central concern

Possible answers:

- use of alliteration/"cup capsizes along the formica".

and/or

- use of onomatopoeia/"with a dull clatter"
- to highlight the loudness of the sound made by the old man/the fact that other customers in the snack bar would have definitely heard his attempts to stand (but do nothing to help)
- use of contrast/"a few heads turn in the crowded evening snack bar" to highlight that though the café was full very few people were prepared to show even the slightest interest in the old man's plight.
- use of simile/"like a monstrous animal caught in a tent"
- to highlight that the old man is seen by others as a terrifying creature
- use of direct speech/"I want – to go to the – toilet" to emphasise that the old man must ask strangers to help with the necessities of life
- use of dashes/"I want – to go to the – toilet" to highlight his uncertainty/anxiety.

42. Candidates should identify the change in the poet's role between stanzas 1 and 2.

In stanza 1 the poet is a mere observer – (his only reference to himself is when he writes "I notice now his stick")

In stanza 2 the poet is a participant – (he is involved in what is going on and experiences first hand the old man's plight)

43. Candidates should comment on two ways in which the poet uses language to emphasise the difficulty of the start of the journey to the toilet.

Possible answers:

- he uses direct speech/"Give me – your arm – it's better" to emphasise the awkwardness of movement

- he says they move "Inch by inch"/reference to repetition which emphasises how slowly they move "a few yards of floor are like a landscape to be negotiated" shows how far it feels they have to travel/difficult crossing the floor is for them

- "drift"/"slow setting out"/"slow dangerous inches" suggests unfocused movement/limited progress/threat .

- he creates a long list of all the obstacles the old man has to cope with which highlights the many everyday objects that are challenging and/or dangerous to the old man

- "concentrate my life to his" emphasises understanding of the challenges faced by the old man.

44. Candidates should show their ability to analyse the poet's characterisation by referring closely and relevantly to the text of this poem and at least one other Morgan poem.

    Possible references:

    In Morgan's **"In the Snack-bar"** the poet creates an interesting character – a vulnerable blind man who relies on the poet's assistance.

    Other interesting characters are presented in **"Trio"** where three individuals, who embody the spirit of Christmas, are walking up Buchanan Street.

    In the opening line of **"Hyena"**, Morgan creates an interesting character. "I am waiting for you" establishes the intimidating nature of the persona. Through Morgan giving the hyena a voice, he brings the character to life by directly addressing the reader.

    "Wait till he sees this but!" – Morgan's use of direct speech in **"Trio"** allows the reader to hear the excitement in the boy's voice as he anticipates the joy he will bring through his gift.

    In **"Good Friday"** the drunk man is an interesting character because he openly acknowledges to a complete stranger his own lack of knowledge about Easter. This allows Morgan to explore the idea of the value of religion in modern society.

    In **"Trio"** all three characters are interesting because through them Morgan explores the central idea of love. He details the objects they carry and celebrates the happiness they radiate.

    Candidates may choose to answer in **bullet points** in this final question, or write a number of linked statements. There is **no requirement** to write a "mini essay".

    Up to 2 marks can be achieved for identifying elements of **commonality** as identified in the question.

    A further 2 marks can be achieved for **reference to the extract given**.

    4 additional marks can be awarded for similar references to **at least one other poem** by the writer.

    <u>In practice this means:</u>

    Identification of commonality (eg: theme, central relationship, importance of setting, use of imagery, development in characterisation, use of personal experience, use of narrative style, or any other key element…)

from the extract:

1 × relevant reference to technique

1 × appropriate comment

or

1 × relevant reference to idea

1 × appropriate comment

or

1 × relevant reference to feature

1 × appropriate comment

or

1 × relevant reference to text

1 × appropriate comment

(maximum of 2 marks only for discussion of extract)

from **at least one other poem by the writer:**

as above (× 2) for **up to 4 marks**

Text 3 – Poetry – *Basking Shark* by Norman MacCaig

45. Incident (1 mark)

    Relevant reference to text (1 mark)

    Reaction (1 mark)

    At sea/rowing/sticks oar in water/disturbs/hits a shark/shark rises up

    and

    disorientated "a rock where none should be"

    or

    threatened "rise with a slounge"

46. Two references (1 mark) with comment (1 mark)

    "not too often though enough" rare occurrence but still prompted reflection

    and/or

    "I count as gain" valuable/thought-provoking experience

    and/or

    "roomsized monster with a/matchbox brain" humorous/not that frightening/insulting

47. Upset/changed/questioned MacCaig's certainty/perspective/view of evolution

    and

    "he shoggled me centuries back" use of humour/made MacCaig think about origins/evolution/life

    or

    "this decadent townee" thinks of his own position culturally

    or

    "Shook on a branch of his family tree" evolution/that they are different/same origin

48. *Possible answers:*

    "Swish up the dirt" disturbance of the water and disturbance of MacCaig's thoughts/views

    or

    "a spring is all the clearer" once water settles, it is clearer as are MacCaig's thoughts/views

or

"I saw me in one fling, emerging from the slime of everything" makes him reflect on his own origins/"slime" – primordial, viscous

49. Candidates should discuss how MacCaig uses personal experience in this poem and in at least one other poem to explore wider themes.

Themes explored through experience:

- the temporariness/insignificance of man
- the relationship between man and other species, man and nature
- the randomness of the process of evolution
- the scale of human evolution vs species which have remained unchanged/unevolved.

Possible references:

"Assisi" The hypocrisy of the church/desensitization to poverty and suffering.

"Aunt Julia" – How lack of common language prevents can be frustrating/prevent communication BUT despite this a real bond between speaker and Aunt is clear. On a wider level, this experience is a comment on the loss of some traditional aspects of Scottish heritage that is in danger of being lost.

"Memorial" – Grief/Permanence, lack of relief from sense of loss/Impact on death and grief on the artistic process.

"Sounds of the Day" – Impact of love and loss on the psyche/Whether experience of relationship worth the pain.

"Visiting Hour" – Death and loss and our own attitudes towards mortality.

Candidates may choose to answer in **bullet points** in this final question, or write a number of linked statements. There is **no requirement** to write a 'mini essay'.

Up to 2 marks can be achieved for identifying elements of **commonality** as identified in the question.

A further 2 marks can be achieved for **reference to the extract given**.

4 additional marks can be awarded for similar references to **at least one other poem** by the writer.

In practice this means:

Identification of commonality (eg: theme, central relationship, importance of setting, use of imagery, development in characterisation, use of personal experience, use of narrative style, or any other key element...)

from the extract:

1 × relevant reference to technique

1 × appropriate comment

or

1 × relevant reference to idea

1 × appropriate comment

or

1 × relevant reference to feature

1 × appropriate comment

or

1 × relevant reference to text

1 × appropriate comment

(maximum of 2 marks only for discussion of extract)

from **at least one other poem by the writer:**

as above (× 2) for **up to 4 marks**

Text 4 – Poetry – *Lucozade* by Jackie Kay

50. Two points for 2 marks:

- Flowers wilt/die. This reminds her of illness/death/ being in hospital.
- Ref to "sad chrysanthemums". Flowers don't make her happy/she thinks they are pointless.
- Lucozade reminds her of past. This brings thoughts of possibility of death.

51. Two references with comment:

- ref to "doctors with their white lies" she doesn't trust doctors/like being in hospital
- ref to "Don't bring magazines, too much about size" she doesn't like media images of women/approve of diets etc
- ref. to "groggy and low" she is down/depressed
- ref to any of "Big brandy … meringue" doesn't approve of diets/she is unconventional/not a stereotypical mother/likes to live for moment/has her own opinions etc
- ref to "luxury" she likes indulgence
- ref to "grapes" she's not keen on conventions/ healthy eating
- ref to "stop the neighbours coming" she is bored/ irritated by neighbours/small talk etc.

52. To be awarded full marks, candidates should identify through references and comments some change – eg sadness to celebration, negative to positive.

Any three references plus acceptable comments for 6 marks.

To gain 6 marks, both sides of change must be dealt with.

- "sad (chrysanthemums)" she is upset
- "weighted (down)" she is burdened/full of negative thoughts

CHANGES TO

- "high hospital bed" girl sees that mother is raised up/not low (connotations of being elevated)
- "light"/"radiant" positive connotations/optimistic
- "billow and whirl" full of life/energy
- "beautiful" admiration, pleasure
- "divine" elevated etc
- "(singing) an old song" good memories of the past

53. Candidates should identify a theme or themes from the poetry of Kay, and be able to show how it is explored in this poem and in at least one other poem by Kay.

Candidates are probably likely to identify one of the following themes:

Illness/death, Family Relationships, Parent/Child relationships

Possible references:

"Bed" – themes of **illness/infirmity/impending death AND/OR mother – daughter relationships**

"Gap Year" – Closeness of parent/child bond.

Candidates may also make reference to the CONTRAST between the obvious bond between the mother and daughter in **"Lucozade"** with the very different exploration of the parent/child relationships considered in **"Divorce"**, **"Keeping Orchids"** and to a lesser extent also in **"Bed"**

Candidates may choose to answer in **bullet points** in this final question, or write a number of linked statements. There is **no requirement** to write a 'mini essay'.

Up to 2 marks can be achieved for identifying elements of **commonality** as identified in the question.

A further 2 marks can be achieved for **reference to the extract given.**

4 additional marks can be awarded for similar references to **at least one other poem** by the writer.

In practice this means:

Identification of commonality (eg: theme, central relationship, importance of setting, use of imagery, development in characterisation, use of personal experience, use of narrative style, or any other key element...)

from the extract:

1 × relevant reference to technique

1 × appropriate comment

or

1 × relevant reference to idea

1 × appropriate comment

or

1 × relevant reference to feature

1 × appropriate comment

or

1 × relevant reference to text

1 × appropriate comment

(maximum of 2 marks only for discussion of extract)

from **at least one other poem by the writer:**

as above (× 2) for **up to 4 marks**

SECTION 2 — Critical Essay

Bands are not grades. The five bands are designed primarily to assist with placing each candidate response at an appropriate point on a continuum of achievement. Assumptions about final grades or association of final grades with particular bands should not be allowed to influence objective assessment.

	20–18	17–14	13–10	9–5	4–0
The candidate demonstrates:	• **a high degree of familiarity** with the text as a whole • **very good understanding** of the central concerns of the text • a line of thought that is **consistently** relevant to the task	• **familiarity** with the text as a whole • **good understanding** of the central concerns of the text • a line of thought that is **relevant** to the task	• **some familiarity** with the text as a whole • **some understanding** of the central concerns of the text • a line of thought that is **mostly relevant** to the task	• **familiarity with some aspects** of the text • **attempts** a line of thought **but this may lack relevance to the task**	Although such essays should be rare, in this category, the candidate's essay will demonstrate one or more of the following • it contains numerous errors in spelling/grammar/ punctuation/ sentence construction/ paragraphing • knowledge and understanding of the text(s) are not used to answer the question • any analysis and evaluation attempted are unconvincing • the answer is simply too thin
Analysis of the text demonstrates:	• **thorough awareness** of the writer's techniques, through analysis, making **confident** use of critical terminology • **very detailed/thoughtful** explanation of stylistic devices supported by a **range of well-chosen** references and/or quotations	• **sound awareness** of the writer's techniques through analysis, making **good** use of critical terminology • **detailed explanation** of stylistic devices supported by **appropriate** references and/ or quotation	• **an awareness** of the writer's techniques through analysis, making **some** use of critical terminology • explanation of stylistic devices supported by **some appropriate** references and/ or quotation	• **some awareness** of **the more obvious** techniques used by the writer • **description of some** stylistic devices followed by limited reference and/or quotation	
Evaluation of the text is shown through:	• **a well developed** commentary of what has been enjoyed/ gained from the text(s), supported by a **range** of well-chosen references to its relevant features	• **a reasonably developed** commentary of what has been enjoyed/ gained from the text (s), supported by **appropriate** references to its relevant features	• **some** commentary of what has been enjoyed/gained from the text(s), supported by **some appropriate** references to its relevant features	• **brief** commentary of what has been enjoyed/gained from the text(s), followed by **brief** reference to its features	
The candidate:	• uses language to communicate a line of thought **very clearly** • uses spelling, grammar, sentence construction and punctuation which are **consistently** accurate • structures the essay **effectively to enhance** meaning/ purpose • uses paragraphing which is **accurate and effective**	• uses language to communicate a line of thought **clearly** • uses spelling, grammar, sentence construction and punctuation which are **mainly** accurate • structures the essay **well** • uses paragraphing which is **accurate**	• uses language to communicate a line of thought **at first reading** • uses spelling, grammar, sentence construction and punctuation which are **sufficiently** accurate • attempts to structure the essay **in an appropriate way** • uses paragraphing which is sufficiently accurate	• uses language to communicate a line of thought which may be disorganised and/or difficult to follow • makes significant errors in spelling/grammar/ sentence construction/ punctuation • has not structured the essay well • has made significant errors in paragraphing	
In summary, the candidates essay is:	thorough and precise	very detailed and shows some insight	fairly detailed and relevant	lacks detail and relevance	superficial and/or technically weak

NATIONAL 5 ENGLISH 2015

READING FOR UNDERSTANDING, ANALYSIS AND EVALUATION

1. Candidates should explain why the first paragraph is an effective opening for the passage.

   Any three points from:

   - It shows/introduces/explains/describes/connects to
   - the idea (fight-flight-freeze)/theme/focus of the text/the rat
   - creates interest/shock/pathos/drama.

   Also accept:

   - reference to second person/"you"
   - with chatty/informal tone
   - single word/minor sentence/short sentence/"Ferociously!"
   - series of short sentences.

2. **Glosses of both words:**

   - "deeply" eg very/completely/profoundly
   - "ingrained" eg embedded/fixed/rooted/established/ intuitive/natural/instinctive/in a long standing fashion.

3. Candidates should explain in their own words two aspects of "danger" or "threat" for two past experiences and two present experiences, from lines 14–21.

   Past – glosses of two:

   - "head-on" eg direct/face to face
   - "regularly" eg frequent
   - "predators …animal" eg creatures (which wanted to harm/kill us)
   - "predators …human kind" eg others like us (wanted to harm/kill us, eg through wars)
   - accept example of predator
   - "to life or limb" eg real physical harm.

   Present – glosses of two:

   - "artificial" eg non-physical/psychological
   - "to ego" eg to pride/self-esteem/vanity
   - "to livelihood" eg to job/earnings
   - "(consequences of) messing up" eg doing it wrong
   - gloss of "taking exam"
   - gloss of "giving a speech"
   - gloss of "taking a penalty".

4. Referring to lines 22–37, candidate should summarise using their own words some of the changes in the body which occur with the response.

   Changes – glosses of:

   - "acceleration of heart … function" eg the heart beats more quickly
   - "acceleration of … lung function" eg breath comes faster
   - "there is paling and flushing" eg the skin changes colour

   - "there is an inhibition of stomach action, such that digestion almost completely ceases" eg the intestines work less
   - "there is a constriction (of blood vessels)" eg (blood vessels) narrow
   - "there is a freeing up of metabolic energy sources (fat and glycogen)" eg feel more energetic
   - "there is a dilation (of the pupils)" eg the eyes widen/expand/enlarge
   - "a relaxation of the bladder" eg waterworks loosen
   - "perception narrows" eg concentration is (more) focused
   - "shaking"/"trembling" eg shuddering or quaking or similar
   - "prime (the muscles)" eg prepare/ready (the muscles)
   - "increase body strength" eg become stronger
   - "increase … blood pressure" eg higher (blood pressure)
   - "(become) hyper-vigilant" eg more alert/pay more attention
   - "(adrenalin) pumping like crazy" eg increase (in adrenalin)
   - "taut" eg tense/tightened
   - "pumped" eg ready.

5. The candidate must offer an explanation on how the sentence "How to deal with these responses?" in line 44 provides an appropriate link at this point of the passage.

   - "These responses" looks back
   - "How"/"to deal" or question (mark) looks forward

   or

   - "These responses" looks back
   - to actions of team-mates or inner dialogue

   or

   - "How"/"to deal" or question (mark) looks forward
   - to identification of strategy (may quote "reflection")

   or

   - reference to the ideas in the text before the link
   - reference to the ideas in the text after the link.

6. By referring to lines 50–54, the candidate must explain **two** examples of the writer's word choice which demonstrate the "benefit" of the response.

   Any two points from:

   - "huge" eg considerable
   - "therapeutic" eg it helps
   - "It takes the edge off" eg it makes us calmer
   - "(It makes a … bewildering reaction) into a comprehensible one" eg (it turns a baffling/puzzling reaction) into one which we understand
   - "liberation" eg freeing
   - "(liberation) from tyranny" eg from oppression
   - "pressure" eg stress.

7. The candidate should explain the attitude of top athletes to pressure, and how two examples of the language used make this attitude clear with reference to lines 55–61.

Identification of attitude, eg pressure can be positive/beneficial.

Possible answers include:

- "paradoxical" /reference to paradox eg emphasises that expectation is worse than reality
- "Pressure is not a problem" eg bluntly states attitude
- "privilege" eg shows that this is something positive
- colon to introduce motto/mantra
- reference to alliteration eg accentuates the positive
- semi-colon after "problem" complements the balance
- balance/(idea of) antithesis of "Pressure ... privilege" draws attention to the bilateral nature
- example(s) cited of famous sportsmen suggests agreement
- "perfectly open" suggests acceptance
- reference to "but" starting sentence emphasises the contrast
- "great pride" emphasises how good they feel
- "facing up to them" shows positive attitude to confronting them
- "they didn't see these ... as signs of weakness" provides a clear statement
- "They created mechanisms" suggests coping strategies
- "grow" emphasises a chance to develop
- "seized (every opportunity)" shows they are keen
- repetition of "They" at the start of a sentence/parallel structure shows affirmative nature of the attitude.

8. The candidate should fully explain using their own words why the advice to "grab" the opportunity might at first seem strange by referring to lines 62–67.

Any three points from:

Then

Glosses of:

- "you will feel uncomfortable" eg you will find it awkward/unpleasant/unnerving
- "your stomach will knot" eg you will feel physically stressed
- "at the moment of truth, you will wish to be anywhere else in the world" eg at the critical/vital time you would wish you were not doing it
- "a nation's expectations on their shoulders" eg much is being hoped for you/pressure is applied/your patriotism is under test.

9. The candidate should pick an expression from the final paragraph (lines 68–71) and show how it helps to contribute to an effective conclusion to the passage.

Reference to an expression from earlier in the article should be made.

Possible answers include:

- "paradoxical" eg repeats word used earlier (line 55)
- "you will grow, learn and mature"eg revisits actual words "grow" (line 56) or "learnt" (line 57) or ideas of athletes profiting from the experience
- "on the football pitch" eg refers back to lines 9–12 or the title
- "in the office" eg refers back to "job interview" (line 45) or "at work" (lines 19–20)
- "fluff your lines" eg refers back to "giving a speech" (line 17)
- "if you miss" eg refers back to "taking a penalty" (line 17).

CRITICAL READING

SECTION 1 – Scottish Text

SCOTTISH TEXT – DRAMA

Text 1 – Drama – *Bold Girls* by Rona Munro

1. Candidates should show an understanding of the key events in this scene. Although the scene is short, many points are revealed here.

Candidates should deal with four separate points.

Possible answers include:

- Marie says she does not know how Cassie coped with Joe's affairs
- Marie displays an idealised view of her relationship with Michael
- Cassie seems to be preparing herself to confess her affair to Marie
- Cassie reacts against her environment
- Marie assures her there are things to look forward to
- Cassie says she is leaving
- Marie is shocked
- Cassie talks about her mother's idealised treatment of the men-folk in prison
- Cassie admits to stealing money from Nora by exploiting her lack of knowledge re the price of fruit
- Cassie shows humour/sarcasm in describing her predicament
- Cassie shows realism
- Marie shows her concern.

2. Candidates should show understanding of the attitudes of Marie.

Marie feels that men can be untrustworthy.

Marie has a romantic/idealised view of her relationship with Michael.

Candidates should refer to the dialogue and quotation is expected to support the argument.

1 mark for relevant quotation selected.

1 mark for appropriate comment about the attitude it reveals.

Possible answers include:

- "I don't know how you coped with all Joe's carry on." plus comment
- "You were the martyr there, Cassie" plus comment
- "I couldn't have stood that, just the lying to you" plus comment

- "It'll tear the heart out of me but tell me, just tell me the truth 'cause I'd want to know." plus comment
- "I never worried." plus comment
- "he was like my best friend" plus comment
- "that's what I miss most. The crack. The sharing." plus comment.

3. Candidates should demonstrate understanding of at least two aspects of Cassie's mood.

   1 mark for selection of relevant reference.

   1 mark for appropriate comment.

   Cassie is in a reflective mood at the start of the extract. Her replies are short and monosyllabic/"It gave me peace."

   She becomes more hesitant/regretful as indicated by the ellipsis/"Marie…"

   She becomes angry and kicks the ground she stands on/"Aw Jesus I hate this place!"/she uses an exclamation

   She makes a stand/she becomes defiant "I'm leaving"

   She is sullen/belligerent She does not elaborate/"Cassie says nothing"

   She complains at length about the way Joe and Martin are treated by Nora. She becomes sarcastic/"…she can spoil them with fruit…"

   Sarcastic/bitter "I'll bring her home something that looks and smells like the Botanic Gardens…"

   She becomes emphatic (about her plans to leave) "I've two hundred pounds saved. I'm going."

   She then criticises herself (for stealing from Nora) "It's desperate isn't it? Thirty-five years old and she's stealing from her mummy's purse."

4. Candidates should discuss the treatment of gender in this extract and in at least one other scene from the play.

   Points likely to be made about women include:

   - Women take care of domestic work
   - They struggle to make ends meet
   - They support their friends
   - They look after the children
   - They do not have the same "social" freedom as men
   - They support their men in prison
   - They live with the threat of paramilitary/domestic violence.

   Points likely to be made about men include:

   - Men are more likely to be imprisoned
   - Men imprisoned for paramilitary activities are highly regarded by their community
   - Men have more "social freedom"
   - Men "con" each other
   - Men do not carry out domestic chores
   - Men are more likely to commit acts of domestic violence.

   Candidates may choose to answer in **bullet points** in this final question, or write a number of linked statements. There is **no requirement** to write a "mini essay".

   Up to 2 marks can be achieved for identifying elements of **commonality** as identified in the question.

A further 2 marks can be achieved for **reference to the extract given.**

4 additional marks can be awarded for similar references to **at least one other text/part of the text** by the writer.

Underline: In practice this means:

Identification of commonality (eg: theme, central relationship, importance of setting, use of imagery, development in characterisation, use of personal experience, use of narrative style, or any other key element…)

from the extract:

1 × relevant reference to technique

1 × appropriate comment

or

1 × relevant reference to idea

1 × appropriate comment

or

1 × relevant reference to feature

1 × appropriate comment

or

1 × relevant reference to text

1 × appropriate comment

(maximum of 2 marks only for discussion of extract)

from **at least one other text/part of the text:**

as above (× 2) for **up to 4 marks**

Text 2 – Drama – *Sailmaker* by Alan Spence

5. Any two points to summarise the situation for one mark each.

   Possible answers include:

   - Alec's mother/Davie's wife has died
   - Alec is beginning to come to terms with his mother's death
   - Davie is struggling to cope with his grief/the death of his wife
   - They are getting the house ready for visitors after the funeral.

6. Candidates should refer to **both** the weather and the setting for full marks.

   1 mark for reference.

   1 mark for comment.

   Possible answers include:

   Weather

   - "breeze was warm"/"the breeze touched my cheek"/"sun shone"/"glinted"/"clouds moving across"
   - Reflects Alec's feeling that his mother has gone to heaven/is safe
   - "wee patch of clear blue"
   - Patch of blue symbolises his mother going to heaven/a sign from her to reassure him.

   Setting

   - "ordinary"/"Nothing had changed" in contrast to the enormity of their loss

- "grey tenements"/"middens ... dustbins ... spilled ashes"/"broken glass"
- Setting is drab/miserable reflects their feelings of despair/depression/bereavement/poverty
- Evidence of rubbish/vandalism suggests lack of care his mother is now in a better place away from here
- "wee boy playing mouth organ"
- Notes on the mouth-organ sound like a bugle call as his mother leaves this world and enters heaven/ reflects feelings of sadness.

7. Candidates should clearly identify how Davie is coping with his current situation.

   Candidates should support their responses with quotation and/or reference.

   1 mark for reference.

   1 mark for comment.

   Possible answers include:

   Supporting evidence:

   - Short sentence(s) to start speech Davie is trying to keep busy to avoid thinking
   - Long sentence with no punctuation reflects Davie's mind – he is trying to do lots of things to avoid stopping and thinking
   - Repetition of "nearly"/2nd time with italics for emphasis suggests he can never actually manage to forget
   - "Christ" use of blasphemy suggests the strength of his feeling
   - Use of 2nd person pronoun "ye"/"you" – to distance himself from situation/make it more general rather than face up to it
   - List of things Davie does reflects him carrying out a number of tasks to avoid thinking
   - "whole minutes" emphasises how often he is thinking about his wife
   - "hit(s) ye" – suggests the almost physical nature of his pain.

8. Candidates should focus on the language used by the characters.

   2 marks for identification of two differences.

   Possible answers include:

   - Alec speaks in English, Davie speaks in Scots
   - Alec's words are in the past tense, Davie's words are in the present tense
   - Alec's words are in sentences, Davie's sentences lack punctuation
   - Alec's sentences are short(er), Davie's are long(er)
   - Alec's sentences are (more) structured, Davie's are (more) unstructured/chaotic
   - Alec's words are more descriptive/poetic, Davie's words are more matter of fact/down to earth
   - Alec's words act as narration, Davie's words act as the speech of a character.

9. Candidates should identify the way the father-son relationship is developed in this extract and elsewhere in the play.

Possible comments from elsewhere include:

- Admiration at start of play
- Spending the bursary money
- Drinking/gambling issues
- Lack of trust
- Neglect/physical abuse
- Acceptance of going separate ways
- Burning yacht etc a resolution/more positive
- Contrast with Billy and Ian's relationship.

Candidates may choose to answer in **bullet points** in this final question, or write a number of linked statements. There is **no requirement** to write a 'mini essay'.

Up to 2 marks can be achieved for identifying elements of **commonality** as identified in the question.

A further 2 marks can be achieved for **reference to the extract** given.

4 additional marks can be awarded for similar references to **at least one other text/part of the text** by the writer.

<u>In practice this means:</u>

Identification of commonality (eg: theme, central relationship, importance of setting, use of imagery, development in characterisation, use of personal experience, use of narrative style, or any other key element...)

from the extract:

1 × relevant reference to technique

1 × appropriate comment

or

1 × relevant reference to idea

1 × appropriate comment

or

1 × relevant reference to feature

1 × appropriate comment

or

1 × relevant reference to text

1 × appropriate comment

(maximum of 2 marks only for discussion of extract)

from **at least one other text/part of the text:**

as above (× 2) for **up to 4 marks**

Text 3 – Drama – *Tally's Blood* by Ann Marie de Mambro

10. Candidates need to cover four separate points to achieve full marks.

    Possible answers include:

    - Her father had arranged for her to marry someone else (Ferdinando, who had a lot of land)
    - Then she met Massimo and fell in love at first sight/ very quickly
    - Her father wouldn't allow it and locked her in a room
    - Massimo climbed up to rescue her
    - They spent the evening together hiding up a tree
    - To deliberately cause a scandal
    - So they would have to be allowed to get married.

11. Candidates should deal with four of the points suggested. For full marks they must show some **change** in Rosinella's thoughts.

1 mark for reference.

1 mark for comment.

Possible answers include:

- At first she is *"Cagey"* suggesting she is reluctant initially
- Then she starts *"Getting into it"* suggesting she is starting to take some pleasure in it
- She is *"Undecided about whether or not to tell"* suggesting she is unsure about what to do
- *"but then does so with glee"* suggesting that she is taking delight in it
- *"Enjoying it now"* suggests she is taking pleasure from it
- *"Mimics the sound"* suggests she is telling the story with some conviction
- By the end she is *"Moved by her story"* suggesting she is completely involved.

12. 1 mark for identification of tone.

1 mark for comment.

Possible tones might include:

nostalgic, romantic, reflective, wistful, humorous, etc.

Any reasonable justification for answer.

13. Candidates are only being asked to identify examples from the extract.

Possible examples include:

"wee", "awfy", "they" (instead of those), "no" (instead of not), "faither", "wean", "hen", "ma" (instead of my).

Any two for 1 mark each.

14. Candidates should discuss how romantic relationships are developed in this extract and elsewhere in the play.

Possible comments from elsewhere include:

- Comment on forbidden relationships
- Lucia and Hughie are childhood friends who end up in a relationship
- Franco and Bridget's difficult relationship
- Rosinella and Massimo's elopement and enduring relationship.

Candidates may choose to answer in **bullet points** in this final question, or write a number of linked statements. There is **no requirement** to write a "mini essay".

Up to 2 marks can be achieved for identifying elements of **commonality** as identified in the question.

A further 2 marks can be achieved for **reference to the extract given.**

4 additional marks can be awarded for similar references to **at least one other text/part of the text** by the writer.

In practice this means:

Identification of commonality (eg: theme, central relationship, importance of setting, use of imagery, development in characterisation, use of personal experience, use of narrative style, or any other key element...)

from the extract:

1 × relevant reference to technique

1 × appropriate comment

or

1 × relevant reference to idea

1 × appropriate comment

or

1 × relevant reference to feature

1 × appropriate comment

or

1 × relevant reference to text

1 × appropriate comment

(maximum of 2 marks only for discussion of extract)

from **at least one other text/part of the text:**

as above (× 2) for **up to 4 marks**

Text 1 – Prose – *The Cone-Gatherers* by Robin Jenkins

15. Any two for one mark each.

Possible answers include:

- sensitive
- gentle
- empathy with animals
- clumsy in his movements (when not in the trees)
- upset.

16. 1 mark for identification.

1 mark for comment.

Possible answers include:

- "Icy sweat of hatred" plus comment
- "His gun aimed at the (feebleminded) hunchback" plus comment
- "The obscene squeal of the killed dwarf" plus comment
- "Noose of disgust and despair" plus comment.

17. 1 mark for any one quotation.

1 mark for comment.

Possible answers include:

- Sea imagery – "sea of branches"/"fantastic sea"/"quiet as fish"/"seaweed"/"submarine monsters" plus comment
- "bronzen brackens" plus comment
- "the overspreading tree of revulsion" plus comment.

18. Candidates must show Duror's feelings before and after.

Before the arrival he felt safe/happy/secure/peaceful/calm, etc there.

After the arrival he felt it had been spoiled/ruined, etc for him.

19. Candidates should discuss how the character of Calum is presented in this extract and elsewhere in the novel.

Possible answers from elsewhere include:

- Calum's gentleness
- Examples of descriptions of Calum's gentleness
- References to Calum's clumsiness when he is not in the trees

- Detailed description of nature (and how it relates to Calum) which occurs throughout the novel.

Candidates may choose to answer in **bullet points** in this final question, or write a number of linked statements. There is **no requirement** to write a "mini essay".

Up to 2 marks can be achieved for identifying elements of **commonality** as identified in the question.

A further 2 marks can be achieved for **reference to the extract given.**

4 additional marks can be awarded for similar references to **at least one other text/part of the text** by the writer.

In practice this means:

Identification of commonality (eg: theme, central relationship, importance of setting, use of imagery, development in characterisation, use of personal experience, use of narrative style, or any other key element...)

from the extract:

1 × relevant reference to technique

1 × appropriate comment

or

1 × relevant reference to idea

1 × appropriate comment

or

1 × relevant reference to feature

1 × appropriate comment

or

1 × relevant reference to text (1)

1 × appropriate comment (1)

(maximum of 2 marks only for discussion of extract)

from **at least one other text/part of the text:**

as above (× 2) for **up to 4 marks**

Text 2 – Prose – *The Testament of Gideon Mack* by James Robertson

20. 1 mark for each identification of aspect.

Possible answers include:

- Two faced/duplicitous
- rebellious
- made himself inconspicuous
- clever/crafty.

21. (a) 1 mark for reference.

1 mark for comment.

Possible answers include:

- "went through with the whole business" suggesting difficulty or hardship or lack of enjoyment
- "a rigorous undertaking" suggesting difficulty or hardship
- "an even greater commitment" suggesting a lot is being asked of him
- "you would have to go a long way...but I did" suggesting his task was harder or that he achieved more than others
- "dissected and deciphered" suggesting the in-depth nature of the work.

(b) 1 mark for reference.

1 mark for comment.

Possible answers include:

- "think of this" – use of command to get the reader's attention/force the reader to consider the task
- repetition of "the nature of" to emphasise the full extent of the task
- listing to emphasise the sheer number of topics covered
- repetition in "many, many hours" to emphasise the time spent on this.

22. 1 mark for comment on the relationship.

1 mark for supporting evidence.

Possible answers include:

- grudging admiration – "respect"
- understanding from Mack – "I was there with him"
- still a lack of closeness between them – "a part of me was keeping its distance".

23. Candidates should discuss how the theme of deception is explored in this extract and elsewhere in the novel.

Possible comments from elsewhere include:

- he became a minister although he doesn't believe in God
- he continues to be hypocritical within his profession
- the first person narration allows the reader to see the inner thoughts versus the outward appearance
- various individual scenes of duplicity throughout the novel, any two examples.

Candidates may choose to answer in **bullet points** in this final question, or write a number of linked statements. There is **no requirement** to write a "mini essay".

Up to 2 marks can be achieved for identifying elements of **commonality** as identified in the question.

A further 2 marks can be achieved for **reference to the extract given.**

4 additional marks can be awarded for similar references to **at least one other text/part of the text** by the writer.

In practice this means:

Identification of commonality (eg: theme, central relationship, importance of setting, use of imagery, development in characterisation, use of personal experience, use of narrative style, or any other key element...)

from the extract:

1 × relevant reference to technique

1 × appropriate comment

or

1 × relevant reference to idea

1 × appropriate comment

or

1 × relevant reference to feature

1 × appropriate comment

or

1 × relevant reference to text

1 × appropriate comment

(maximum of 2 marks only for discussion of extract)

from **at least one other text/part of the text:**

as above (× 2) for **up to 4 marks**

Text 3 — Prose — *Kidnapped* by Robert Louis Stevenson

24. Four points to be made.

    One mark for each point.

    Possible answers include:

    - David arrives in/near Edinburgh
    - David asks for directions to Cramond
    - David sees/hears the redcoats
    - David asks/talks to a man with a cart about the house of Shaws
    - David receives negative response from the carter
    - David asks/talks to a barber about the house of Shaws
    - David receives negative response from the barber
    - David is left concerned.

25. There should be an understanding that David believes that it is the juxtaposition between his simple, grubby clothes which jarred with his asking about – what he thought was – a grand house such as the Shaws.

    A gloss of:

    "At first I thought the plainness of my appearance, in my country habit, and that all dusty from the road," (1 mark)

    "consorted ill with the greatness of the place to which I was bound." (1 mark)

26. (a) 1 mark for statement of mood in opening paragraph.

    1 mark for example of writer's use of language in opening paragraph.

    1 mark for comment on language.

    Possible answers include:

    - mood – optimistic, happy, content, etc.

    Word choice:

    - "pleasure" have a great liking/desire
    - "wonder" – as to marvel at a great spectacle
    - "beheld" – to observe something of great impact
    - "pride" delight/joy at the sight
    - "merry (music)" – joyful/happy.

    Metaphor:

    - "the pride of life seemed to mount into my brain" to be at the forefront of the mind/to be directly connected to the mind in a powerful way.

    Alliteration:

    - "merry music" repeated "m" sound has a length which pleasant, soft, jaunty and childlike in its alliterative use.

    (b) 1 mark for statement of mood in final paragraph.

    1 mark for example of writer's use of language in final paragraph.

    1 mark for comment on language.

    Possible answers include:

    - mood – pessimistic, confused, perturbed, etc.

Word choice:

- "illusions" – deceptive/misconception
- "indistinct" – unclear
- "accusations" – negative connotations of illegal actions
- "fancy" imagination not reality
- "start and stare" showing shock at the mention of Shaws (also could award marks for the sharp alliterative effect of the sibilance)
- "ill-fame" – of poor reputation.

Metaphor:

- "the blow this dealt to my illusions" – affected almost physically/violently as with a blow.

Sentence structure:

- use of two questions/placement of questions at end of paragraph emphasising doubt and confusion/climactic nature.

27. Candidates should discuss the development of David Balfour's character in this extract and elsewhere in the novel.

    Possible comments from elsewhere include:

    - becomes more adventurous
    - becomes more experienced
    - becomes more confident
    - any two specific points in the novel which show his development.

    Candidates may choose to answer in **bullet points** in this final question, or write a number of linked statements. There is **no requirement** to write a "mini essay".

    Up to 2 marks can be achieved for identifying elements of **commonality** as identified in the question.

    A further 2 marks can be achieved for **reference to the extract given.**

    4 additional marks can be awarded for similar references to **at least one other text/part of the text** by the writer.

    In practice this means:

    Identification of commonality (eg: theme, central relationship, importance of setting, use of imagery, development in characterisation, use of personal experience, use of narrative style, or any other key element...)

    from the extract:

    1 × relevant reference to technique

    1 × appropriate comment

    or

    1 × relevant reference to idea

    1 × appropriate comment

    or

    1 × relevant reference to feature

    1 × appropriate comment

    or

    1 × relevant reference to text

    1 × appropriate comment

    (maximum of 2 marks only for discussion of extract)

from **at least one other text/part of the text:**

as above (× 2) for **up to 4 marks**

Text 4 – Prose – *Mother and Son* by Iain Crichton Smith

28. Candidates should give 4 relevant points for 1 mark each.

    Possible answers include:

    - Constantly ridicules him – "always laughed at him"
    - Picks on him/highlights his faults persistently – "pecked cruelly at his defences"
    - Hates the power she has over him despite her frailty – "What is she anyway?"/"How can this thing....?"
    - Anger that she uses illness as a reason to behave as she does – "She's been ill...doesn't excuse her"
    - Anger that she is destroying his life – "she's breaking me up"
    - Also his chances of a life in the future – "if she dies...good for anyone."
    - Blames her for his loneliness/isolation from his peers – "shivered inside his loneliness"/"That would be the boys...".

29. 1 mark for reference.

    1 mark for comment.

    Possible examples/explanations:

    - "face had sharpened itself... quickness"/"pecking at....cruelly at his defences" – emphasises her sharpness/although small and frail like a bird has the capacity to destroy him
    - "some kind of animal"/"this thing" – makes her seem less than human
    - "breaking me up" – idea that she is destroying him
    - Description of his angry actions shows his feelings
    - "abrupt"/"savage"/shaking with anger towards her/"rage shook him" shows how angry he is
    - Use of questions/"How can this thing..."/"What is she anyway?" Emphasise the hateful thoughts he has towards her.

30. 1 mark for reference.

    1 mark for comment.

    Possible examples/explanations:

    - (sense of loneliness) "closed around him" feels engulfed by loneliness
    - "on a boat on the limitless ocean" feels adrift and alone in an endless sea
    - (compares this to his own home) "just as his house was on a limitless moorland" – gives sense of isolation.

31. 1 mark for reference.

    1 mark for comment.

    Possible answers include:

    - "Remember to clean the tray tomorrow"/mother's words are seen as provocative
    - "fighting back the anger" suggests rising emotion
    - "swept over him" overwhelming feelings
    - "He turned back to the bed." – it's a dramatic moment
    - (Repetition of) "smash" suggestion of potential violence

    - (Repetition of) "there was" creation of drama
    - Final short sentence makes for dramatic ending.

32. Candidates should discuss a character's realisation in this extract as well as at least one other character's realisation from at least one other story.

    Possible comments from other stories include:

    'The Telegram' – true destination of telegram, more understanding between the two women

    'The Red Door' – realisation of sense of freedom for main character

    'In Church' – realisation of futility of war

    'The Painter' – realisation of unpleasantness of community.

    Candidates may choose to answer in **bullet points** in this final question, or write a number of linked statements. There is **no requirement** to write a "mini essay".

    Up to 2 marks can be achieved for identifying elements of **commonality** as identified in the question.

    A further 2 marks can be achieved for **reference to the extract given.**

    4 additional marks can be awarded for similar references to **at least one other text/part of the text** by the writer.

    In practice this means:

    Identification of commonality (2) (eg: theme, central relationship, importance of setting, use of imagery, development in characterisation, use of personal experience, use of narrative style, or any other key element...)

    from the extract:

    1 × relevant reference to technique

    1 × appropriate comment

    or

    1 × relevant reference to idea

    1 × appropriate comment

    or

    1 × relevant reference to feature

    1 × appropriate comment

    or

    1 × relevant reference to text

    1 × appropriate comment

    (maximum of 2 marks only for discussion of extract)

    from **at least one other text/part of the text:**

    as above (× 2) for **up to 4 marks**

Text 5 – Prose – *All That Glisters* by Anne Donovan

33. Four separate points for one mark each.

    Possible answers include:

    - The family prepare for the funeral
    - Father's body put in parents' bedroom
    - Girl asked if she wants to see body
    - Girl has mixed feelings about seeing the body
    - Girl feels her mother is acting aloof
    - Girl gets dressed for funeral
    - Auntie Pauline reacts badly to girl's choice of outfit

- Memory of wearing dress for father
- Memory of father's approval.

34. 1 mark for reference.

1 mark for comment.

Possible answers include:

- "blur" unclear/many things happening/movement
- Movement of people "comin and goin" busy/confusing
- ("makin sandwiches" and "pourin oot glasses of whisky") for "men in overcoats" whom she doesn't recognise, perhaps distant or seldom seen relatives
- "makin sandwiches"/"pourin oot glasses of whisky" suggests endless hospitality
- reference to listing or use of commas suggests confusion of events or lack of clarity.

35. 1 mark for identification of feature.

Possible answers include:

- (Repeated) use of first person
- Use of parenthesis
- Use of question
- Use of Scots
- Use of colloquial language
- Long/rambling sentences.

36. 1 mark for reference.

1 mark for comment.

Possible answers include:

- "her face froze over" shows her disgust/astonishment
- Use of (rhetorical) question/"Whit the hell do you think you're daein?" shows shock/disapproval
- Use of (expletive)/"hell" shows anger
- Use of imperatives/"Go...get changed" shows her disapproval of the outfit
- Instructions/commands/insistence show her disapproval.

37. Candidates should discuss how the theme of relationships is explored in this extract and in at least one other story by Donovan.

Possible comments from other stories include:

'A Chitterin' Bite' – breakdown of two relationships, loss of friendship etc

'Zimmerobics' – relationships across generations

'Dear Santa'/'Away in a Manger' – mother-daughter relationships

Candidates may choose to answer in **bullet points** in this final question, or write a number of linked statements. There is **no requirement** to write a "mini essay".

Up to 2 marks can be achieved for identifying elements of **commonality** as identified in the question.

A further 2 marks can be achieved for **reference to the extract given.**

4 additional marks can be awarded for similar references to **at least one other text/part of the text** by the writer.

<u>In practice this means:</u>

Identification of commonality (eg: theme, central relationship, importance of setting, use of imagery, development in characterisation, use of personal experience, use of narrative style, or any other key element...)

from the extract:

1 × relevant reference to technique

1 × appropriate comment

or

1 × relevant reference to idea

1 × appropriate comment

or

1 × relevant reference to feature

1 × appropriate comment

or

1 × relevant reference to text

1 × appropriate comment

(maximum of 2 marks only for discussion of extract)

from **at least one other text/part of the text:**

as above (× 2) for **up to 4 marks**

Text 1 — Poetry — *Valentine* by Carol Ann Duffy

38. Two marks can be awarded for two main ideas or concerns shown in first two lines.

Only one mark should be awarded for one main idea or concern.

Possible answers include:

- (The unsatisfactory nature of) traditional Valentine gifts
- The rejection of a clichéd/conventional view of love
- Offering of an alternative
- The need to be honest/truthful about love
- The importance of recognising the mundane/unpleasant aspects of love.

39. Four marks can be awarded for two examples of language used to create a positive view of love.

1 mark for example.

1 mark for comment.

Possible answers include:

- The word choice of "moon" suggests romance/is a conventional romantic symbol
- The word choice of "promised" suggests commitment/guarantee that love will flourish
- The word choice of "light" links to "moon" to reinforce romantic associations/has positive connotations linked to goodness or truth
- The word choice of "careful" has connotations of tenderness
- The comparison of removing the skin of an onion to "undressing" adds seductive/sexual element.

40. Two marks can be awarded for one example of language used to create a negative view of love.

1 mark for example.

1 mark for comment.

Possible answers include:

- "blind you with tears" suggests upset/pain

- "blind" suggests the distortion/lack of clarity cc
- "a wobbling photo of grief" suggests unsettling/ distorting nature of love Accept comments on "photo" or "grief" itself
- The personification of "kiss" as "fierce"/word choice of "fierce" suggests danger/threat/aggression
- "will stay on your lips" (to suggest the lingering taste of the onion) suggests the difficulty of escaping a relationship
- The word choice of "possessive" suggests jealousy/ desire to control
- The juxtaposition of "possessive" and "faithful" undermines the normally positive view of commitment
- The inclusion/qualification of "for as long" suggests that the commitment will not last.

41. Candidates should show understanding of the term "conclusion" and how the content of the last stanza continues ideas and/or language from the earlier stanzas.

    2 marks for reference to the final stanza referring back to earlier in the poem.

    Possible answers include:

    - (The imperative) "Take it" continues the portrayal of the speaker as commanding/insistent
    - (The imperative) "Take it" concludes a series of imperatives to suggest the listener's reluctance to accept the gift
    - "platinum" suggests the enduring value of love (despite the negative features highlighted)
    - "loops" suggests never ending commitment/ constraint/control highlighted earlier
    - "shrink" reinforces the claustrophobic/constraining nature of marriage
    - The comparison of the inner rings of the onion to a "wedding ring" continues the subverting of conventional symbols of love/reinforces the constraining nature of marriage
    - The parody of a wedding proposal in " if you like "continues the subverting of conventional romantic symbols
    - The positioning of "Lethal" in a line of its own/the word choice of "Lethal" develops/reinforces previous examples of aggression
    - "cling"/repetition of "cling" links back to the "possessive" nature of love mentioned earlier
    - "knife" reinforces love as menacing or dangerous.

42. Candidates should show awareness of the ideas and/or language of this poem and at least one other poem by Duffy.

    Possible comments from other poems include:

    "Havisham" – pain of relationship breaking down

    "Originally" – relationship with environment/identity/ self-knowledge

    "Ann Hathaway" – sexual relationship

    "War Photographer" – photographer's relationship with work/material

    "Mrs Midas" – breakdown in relationship/memories of good times.

Candidates may choose to answer in **bullet points** in this final question, or write a number of linked statements. There is **no requirement** to write a "mini essay".

Up to 2 marks can be achieved for identifying elements of **commonality** as identified in the question.

A further 2 marks can be achieved for **reference to the extract given.**

4 additional marks can be awarded for similar references to **at least one other text/part of the text** by the writer.

<u>In practice this means:</u>

Identification of commonality (eg: theme, central relationship, importance of setting, use of imagery, development in characterisation, use of personal experience, use of narrative style, or any other key element…)

from the extract:

1 × relevant reference to technique

1 × appropriate comment

or

1 × relevant reference to idea

1 × appropriate comment

or

1 × relevant reference to feature

1 × appropriate comment

or

1 × relevant reference to text

1 × appropriate comment

(maximum of 2 marks only for discussion of extract)

from **at least one other text/part of the text:**

as above (× 2) for **up to 4 marks**

Text 2 — Poetry — *Hyena* by Edwin Morgan

43. For full marks answers should make two clear points.

    One mark for each point. Own words required.

    Possible answers include:

    - Hyena is patient
    - Hyena is dangerous/threatening
    - Hyena is self-obsessed
    - Hyena is hungry and thirsty
    - Hunger makes hyena more threatening
    - Hyena must not be underestimated
    - Hyena may appear to be asleep but can pounce at any time.

44. Two references plus comments on two features used by the writer in these lines.

    1 mark for reference.

    1 mark for comment.

    Possible answers include:

    - "I have a rough coat" or "with dark spots like the bush-tufted plains of Africa" or "a shaggy bundle" – he is inelegant/scruffy
    - "crafty" he is sly/clever
    - "I sprawl ... of gathered energy" eg he appears to be relaxed but is ready to pounce

- "I lope, I slaver" – he is ungainly/clumsy
- The list describes the hyena's movement, etc
- "I am a ranger" he scans the landscape for dead animals
- Reference to "I eat the dead" eg he profits by feeding on creatures already dead/lacks the dignity or skill of a hunter, etc
- Use of short sentences suggests threatening nature of hyena/his grim certainty, etc
- Use of repetition suggests threatening nature, etc
- Use of question suggests apparent confidence of hyena, etc.

45. 1 mark for reference to feature.

    1 mark for comment relating to tense, menacing atmosphere.

    Possible answers include:

    - Use of questions to emphasise the hyena's slyness or power
    - Use of euphemism as the hyena calls his howl his "song"
    - Reference to aspects of setting/background, eg "moon pours hard and cold" suggests eerie place
    - Use of short sentences to increase tension
    - Conversational tone eg "Would you meet me there in the waste places?" creating false sense of friendliness
    - "my golden supper" is a macabre image
    - "I am not laughing" is a chilling statement
    - "crowd of fangs" is threatening/dangerous
    - "I am not laughing" could be seen as a threat/warning.

46. For 2 marks, candidates should refer to a feature of the last stanza and show how it effectively continues an idea/language feature from earlier in the poem.

    Possible answers include:

    - "I am waiting" repeats opening line/reiterates that the hyena is always ready to feed on carrion/gives the poem a cyclical structure
    - "I am crouching ... till you are ready for me" recalls the hyena lying in wait in stanza one
    - "My place is to pick you clean and leave your bones to the wind" brings the references to "you" throughout the poem to a macabre climax.

47. Candidates should show understanding of how Morgan uses word choice and/or imagery effectively to create a striking visual impression or scene in this poem and in at least one other poem.

    Possible comments on other poems include:

    "Good Friday" – clear sense of scene comes across with several visual references to the journey of the bus ("brakes violently," "lurches round into the sun," etc)

    "In the snack bar" – many references to place/scene throughout the poem

    "Trio" – winter/Christmas scene established through expressions such as "sharp winter evening," "under the Christmas lights," etc

    "Winter" – many references to place/scene throughout the poem

    "Slate" – many references to place/scene throughout the poem.

Candidates may choose to answer in **bullet points** in this final question, or write a number of linked statements. There is **no requirement** to write a "mini essay".

Up to 2 marks can be achieved for identifying elements of **commonality** as identified in the question.

A further 2 marks can be achieved for **reference to the extract given.**

4 additional marks can be awarded for similar references to **at least one other text/part of the text** by the writer.

In practice this means:

Identification of commonality (eg: theme, central relationship, importance of setting, use of imagery, development in characterisation, use of personal experience, use of narrative style, or any other key element...)

from the extract:

1 × relevant reference to technique

1 × appropriate comment

or

1 × relevant reference to idea

1 × appropriate comment

or

1 × relevant reference to feature

1 × appropriate comment

or

1 × relevant reference to text

1 × appropriate comment

(maximum of 2 marks only for discussion of extract)

from **at least one other text/part of the text:**

as above (× 2) for **up to 4 marks**

Text 3 — Poetry — *Visiting Hour* **by Norman MacCaig**

48. 1 mark for reference.

    1 mark for comment.

    Possible answers include:

    - "The hospital smell combs my nostrils" suggests visit is familiar/unpleasant/overpowering smell/vivid sensory image
    - "green and yellow corridors" suggests he finds visit unpleasant – connotations of colours/vivid sensory image
    - "What seems a corpse" suggests he feels uncertainty/anxiety about visit
    - "trundled" suggests he feels the patient is being treated impersonally/dehumanised
    - "vanishes" suggests he is very aware of death as absolute/final
    - "heavenward" suggests he is very aware of finality of death/religious questions
    - "I will not feel, I will not feel, until I have to"/repetition here tries to delay/avoid emotions.

49. 1 mark for technique.

    1 mark for comment.

    Possible answers include:

    - "walk lightly, swiftly" – repetition of adverbs admires nurses' ability to deal with stresses of nursing

- "here and up and down and there" – unusual word order lightens mood/emphasises number/activity of nurses
- "their slender waists miraculously carrying their burden" – word-choice/metaphor admires nurses' ability to deal with stresses/burden despite being small/light
- "miraculously" – word choice – religious connotations poet thinks nurses are angelic/have magical powers
- "so much pain, so/many deaths …/so many farewells" – Repetition of "so" suggests admiration for nurses who have to deal with pain and death frequently.

50. 1 mark for reference.

1 mark for comment.

Possible answers include:

- "white cave of forgetfulness" or gloss suggests curtains or sheets are impenetrable/patient is isolated or ignored/poet is excluded/patient herself cannot remember things
- "withered hand/trembles on its stalk" or gloss woman's body is dying/frail/weak
- "Eyes move behind eyelids too heavy to raise" or gloss impersonal description/suggests how ill/weak patient is
- "Arm wasted of colour" or gloss arm is pale, lifeless, useless, no longer functioning
- "glass fang" or gloss suggests vampire-like IV, emphasising the poet's grief and distress
- "not guzzling but giving" or gloss alliteration suggests poet first sees the transfusion as pointless but then realises it is keeping patient alive.

51. Candidates should discuss MacCaig's use of imagery in this poem and in at least one other poem.

Possible comments from other poems include:

"Assisi" – appropriate comments on eg "half-filled sack"; "clucking contentedly", etc

"Memorial" – appropriate comments on eg "carousel of language"; "sad music", etc

"Basking Shark" – appropriate comments on eg "tin-tacked with rain"; "roomsized monster with a matchbox brain", etc

"Sounds of the Day" – "black drums rolled"; "bangle of ice round your wrist", etc

"Aunt Julia" – "she was buckets"; "with a seagull's voice", etc.

Candidates may choose to answer in **bullet points** in this final question, or write a number of linked statements. There is **no requirement** to write a "mini essay".

Up to 2 marks can be achieved for identifying elements of **commonality** as identified in the question.

A further 2 marks can be achieved for **reference to the extract given.**

4 additional marks can be awarded for similar references to **at least one other text/part of the text** by the writer.

In practice this means:

Identification of commonality (eg: theme, central relationship, importance of setting, use of imagery, development in characterisation, use of personal experience, use of narrative style, or any other key element…)

from the extract:

1 × relevant reference to technique

1 × appropriate comment

or

1 × relevant reference to idea

1 × appropriate comment

or

1 × relevant reference to feature

1 × appropriate comment

or

1 × relevant reference to text

1 × appropriate comment

(maximum of 2 marks only for discussion of extract)

from **at least one other text/part of the text:**

as above (× 2) for **up to 4 marks**

Text 4 – Poetry – *Divorce* by Jackie Kay

52. Candidates can refer to meaning or to techniques.

Two references to meaning 1 mark each.

1 mark for reference to technique.

1 mark for comment.

Possible answers include:

- She did not make a vow to stay together
- As her parents had done
- She wants out now
- She uses an emphatic tone
- She uses monosyllabic words
- She uses enjambment
- She uses a cliché
- She uses an ironic tone
- She uses negative language.

53. Candidates should make 3 distinct points for 3 marks.

Possible answers include:

- Gloss of "you never, ever said/a kind word" – mother was not positive/encouraging to her
- Gloss of "or a thank-you" – mother was ungrateful
- "tedious chores" – parents made the persona do hard/demanding housework
- "your breath smells like a camel," etc – father was (personally) repulsive
- "Are you in the cream puff," etc – father made sarcastic comments
- "Lady muck" – father put her down
- "I'd be better off in an orphanage" – emphasises how bad they are.

54. 1 mark for reference.

1 mark for comment.

Possible answers include:

- "faces turn up to the light" "(turn) up" **or** "light" suggest positivity, enlightenment

- "who speak in the soft murmur of rivers" suggests calmness/quiet
- "and never shout" suggests calm, quiet approach
- "stroke their children's cheeks" suggests love/gentleness/caring
- "sing in the colourful voices of rainbows, red to blue" suggests brightness/enjoyment/happiness/beauty/varied approach, etc.

55. 1 mark for identification of tone.

1 mark for reference.

1 mark for comment.

Possible answers include:

Humour:

- "and quickly" – persona can't wait to get away from parents
- "your breath smells like a camel" humorously unappealing/exaggeration/further reference to "gives me the hump"
- "I would be better off in an orphanage" – humorous exaggeration.

Despair:

- reference to "there are things I cannot suffer any longer" – persona is at end of tether.

Anger:

- "I never chose you" – persona is angry with parents/fact that she is trapped.

Dismissive:

- reference to "I don't want to be your child"/"These parents are not you"/"not you" persona rejects parents.

Admiration:

- reference to "There are parents whose faces turn up to the light"/"There are parents who stroke their children's cheeks"/"sing in the colourful voices of rainbows", etc, the persona admires these parents and wishes hers could be more like them.

Any other reasonable identification of a tone, plus reference, plus comment.

56. Candidates should discuss the theme of family relationships in this poem and at least one other poem by Jackie Kay.

Possible comments on other poems include:

"My Grandmother's Houses" – girl/grandmother

"Lucozade" – mother/daughter

"Gap Year" – mother/daughter

"Bed" – mother/daughter

"Keeping Orchids" – mother/daughter

Candidates may choose to answer in **bullet points** in this final question, or write a number of linked statements. There is **no requirement** to write a "mini essay".

Up to 2 marks can be achieved for identifying elements of **commonality** as identified in the question.

A further 2 marks can be achieved for **reference to the extract given.**

4 additional marks can be awarded for similar references to **at least one other text/part of the text** by the writer.

In practice this means:

Identification of commonality (eg: theme, central relationship, importance of setting, use of imagery, development in characterisation, use of personal experience, use of narrative style, or any other key element…)

from the extract:

1 × relevant reference to technique

1 × appropriate comment

or

1 × relevant reference to idea

1 × appropriate comment

or

1 × relevant reference to feature

1 × appropriate comment

or

1 × relevant reference to text

1 × appropriate comment

(maximum of 2 marks only for discussion of extract)

from **at least one other text/part of the text:**

as above (× 2) for **up to 4 marks**

SECTION 2 – Critical Essay

Please see the assessment criteria for the Critical Essay on page 131.

NATIONAL 5 ENGLISH
2016

READING FOR UNDERSTANDING, ANALYSIS AND EVALUATION

1. Any two points for 1 mark each.

   Glosses of:

   - "follow in the footsteps of Diana Ross and Whitney Houston" eg she was a great (female) singer/star too
   - "belt out" eg give a powerful delivery
   - "the voice of Elsa"/"the most successful animated film ..." eg she was the singer of the hit film/song
   - "ubiquitous" eg the song was heard everywhere (accept eg "was well known")
   - "Oscar-winning" eg the song was critically acclaimed
   - "more than three million copies sold" eg the song was (very) popular/profitable
   - "(more than passing) acquaintance" eg she has (good) experience "with anthems" eg of important/highly-regarded songs

2. 1 mark for reference; 1 mark for comment.

   - "stratospheric" eg suggests signal/immense/far-reaching/heightened achievement/out of this world
   - "(takings of more than) £800 million" OR "it's No 5 in the all-time list of highest-grossing films" OR uses statistics eg to show that the film has made a great deal of money
   - uses parenthesis to include (significant) statistics/evidence
   - "has elevated her" eg she has achieved greater prominence
   - "into a new league" eg into a different (superior) context

3. Any five points.

   Glosses of:

   - "she has clearly been reprimanded" eg they have a system of discipline/control
   - "by the Disney suits" eg they are conventionally dressed (ie reference to appearance)
   - "by the Disney suits" eg conservative/corporate/faceless (ie reference to attitude/mindset)
   - "Apparently I spoke out of turn" eg they disliked dissent
   - "Disney doesn't have sequels, (so it would be a first if there was one)" eg they don't (usually) produce follow-up films
   - "stage show" OR "six-minute short" OR "new song" indicates eg (commercial) versatility
   - "(much) mooted" eg Disney is the centre of speculation
   - "the Disney people keep things close to their chests" OR "tight-lipped" eg they are secretive/they say little
   - "happy to milk the commercial opportunities" OR "enjoyed a mighty bump" eg they take pleasure in exploiting/maximising the financial gain

4. 1 mark for reference; 1 mark for comment (x2).

   - "There to be shot at" eg suggests people's readiness to denigrate OR (image of) "shot at" illustrates eg the critics' aggression/hostility/targeting
   - "criticised" eg indicates open to negative comment
   - "failing to hit a high note" eg suggest harshness of criticism
   - parenthetical insertion (of "singing in sub-zero temperatures") eg serves to highlight the point
   - substance of "sub-zero temperatures" eg adverse conditions
   - "still some who noticed the odd flat note" eg suggests (excessive) vigilance of audience/inability to please everyone
   - "The unnerving" eg it is scary
   - "proximity" eg the footballers are close
   - "of several dozen" eg there are many of them
   - "hulking (American footballers)" OR "huge" eg they are very big/intimidating
   - "strong presence (these athletes have)" eg they have an aura/charisma
   - "you're this one woman, singing on her own" eg she was alone/an outnumbered female
   - "(they're so ...) daunting" eg (the men are) intimidating
   - use of ellipsis suggests she wants to be precise in her own comments/provides a dramatic pause/emphasises "daunting"

5. Any one pair OR two correct selections covering different directions.

   - "One woman" looks back to "one woman" OR "on her own" OR the idea of isolation
   - "squad of men" looks back to "several dozen hulking" OR "huge" OR "American footballers" OR the idea of male physical presence
   - "Frozen" looks forward to "Disney animation"
   - "a feminist breakthrough" looks forward to (idea of) "The first ... to be directed ... by a woman" OR "love ... between two sisters" OR "not because some Prince Charming is saving the day"
   - "One woman opposite a squad of men" (accept paraphrase) looks back to the isolation of Idina Menzel
   - information before colon looks back information after colon looks forward

6. 1 mark for reference; 1 mark for comment (x2).

   - "heroine" eg strength of character
   - "subtle" eg not straightforward
   - "conflicted" eg has contradictory emotions/internal battles/complications
   - "sorceress" eg supernatural
   - "struggling to control her powers" eg has difficulties with her abilities
   - "she keeps [Anna] at a distance" eg deliberately remote
   - "for fear of turning her into a popsicle" eg she wields (potentially harmful) power

- "(grandiose) sulks" eg is (spectacularly) moody
- "emo (princess)" eg alternative/sensitive/of dark mind or appearance/saturnine
- "(definitely) complicated" eg (undeniably) complex
- "not stereotypes" eg not predictable/what is conventionally expected

7. • her sister's company (beautifully) encapsulated key ideas of the films
   - **OR** Travolta's error heightened her profile
   - **OR** the song was up for (and won) an (top) award – "Oscar" may be lifted and she got to sing it

8. It is possible to gain full marks through examination of one linguistic aspect.

   Sentence structure:
   - long compared to short sentences **OR** appropriate contrasting references shows complexity compared simplicity

   Tone:
   - appropriate contrasting references eg "several zeitgeist-y things across different generations"/"people who are trying to find themselves" compared with "one more (burning) question"/"No I do not!" shows formality/seriousness compared to lightness/humour/vehemence

   Word choice:
   - "zeitgeist-y" **OR** "resonate" compared to "Does she have her own Elsa dress" shows the difference between difficulty and simplicity
   - "proud" and "much to learn" exhibits the difference between self-esteem and humility
   - "Rent to Wicked" **OR** "Glee to Frozen" illustrates then and now
   - "Frozen" and "burning". Comment must show understanding these are antonyms
   - "certainly aware" and "I have as much to learn myself". Comment must show understanding these are antonymous

9. *Any five from:*

Reference to	Glossed by (eg)
"I spoke out of turn"	She can be forthright/impulsive
"I'd have to play Elsa's mother, probably" or "she laughs"	She has a (self-deprecating) sense of humour
"she sounds slightly disappointed"	She likes to be the star/centre of attention/is self-centred
Despite criticisms	She shows persistence
"they're … daunting"	She can be intimidated
"not because some Prince Charming is saving the day"	She is assertive/feminist (accept slang)
"It was Cara whom Menzel took as her date"	She is close to/fond of her sister/caring
"wincingly"	She is modest/embarrassed by her sister's admiration

Reference to	Glossed by (eg)
"she … recognises … Travolta's slip"	She is perceptive/realistic
"her conversation is a mix of Broadway-speak"	She can be/is shrewd enough to adapt to her environment/use platitudes
"battled-hardened"	She is tough/resilient
"ambition"	She has aspirations
"aware of the value of appearing"	She is shrewd/pragmatic
"I'm proud of that"	She relishes fans' identification with her
"I have as much to learn myself"	She is modest/self-aware
"I don't look that good as a blonde"	She is modest NB please don't credit 'modest' twice
"she'd also quite enjoy ruling over her own wintry kingdom"	She enjoys power/dominance/prominence

CRITICAL READING

SECTION 1 – SCOTTISH TEXT

PART A – DRAMA – *Bold Girls* by Rona Munro

1. Any three key points for 1 mark each.

   Candidates are expected to use their own words.

   Possible answers include:
   - Deirdre confronts Marie about the truth about Michael (her father)
   - Marie tries to avoid telling her the truth
   - Marie (loses her temper) and destroys the photograph of Michael
   - Marie sees Deirdre's bruises and asks about them
   - there is temporary physical closeness between the women
   - the women start to face up to the truth about Michael (and his affairs)
   - there is an increasing sense of understanding between the women by the end of the extract

2. 1 mark for reference; 1 mark for comment (x2).

   Possible answers include:
   - Marie is angry "Marie doesn't turn"
   - Marie is shocked "Marie turns startled"
   - Marie loses control of her emotions "… laugh hysterically"
   - Marie is frightened "Marie backs off a step"
   - Marie loses her temper "Suddenly Marie flies at her"

3. Candidates should make some of the following possible observations:
   - she destroys Michael's photograph which is surprising as it has been a symbol of her adulation/has dominated the setting/staging
   - she is aggressive in destroying the photograph which is surprising because she is usually calm
   - she immediately tidies up which is surprising because she seems to accept this as "closure"/returns to domestic role

4. Candidates should identify one attitude towards Marie (for 1 mark).

   Candidates should select a relevant piece of dialogue (for 1 mark) and explain fully how this conveys the attitude (for 1 mark).

   Possible answers include:

   - **Identification of attitude:** Deirdre is at points surprised/confused/upset/aggressive/calm/inquisitive
   - "But you'd know…" seeks the truth
   - "here, that's you got everything back" implies resentment
   - "I want the truth out of you. I mean it." short sentences gives emphatic tone/impatience/assertiveness
   - "Tell me!" exclamation/monosyllabic words indicate(s) impatience
   - "Just the fella she's got living with her just now." indicates she is accepting/philosophical about being a victim of domestic violence

5. Candidates should identify areas of conflict in the characters' lives from this scene and elsewhere in the play.

   Possible areas for comment include:

   - Marie and Deirdre seem to resolve their conflict as an understanding is reached between them by the end of the play.
   - Cassie and Nora's conflict grows as Cassie's plan to move away is revealed and she does not accept the truth about her father.
   - There is ongoing political conflict in the world beyond the immediate setting of the play.
   - There is conflict between the characters and their bleak setting. There are continued references to the blandness/drabness of the setting.
   - Conflict between men and women is a feature of the play. There are several examples of ongoing clashes between stereotypical male and female behaviour.
   - There is conflict between Cassie and Marie over the issue of infidelity.
   - Reference to the knife being a symbol of conflict.

   Candidates may choose to answer in **bullet points** in this final question, or write a number of linked statements. There is **no requirement** to write a "mini essay".

   Up to 2 marks can be achieved for identifying elements of commonality as requested in the question. A further 2 marks can be achieved for **reference to the extract given**.

   4 additional marks can be awarded for similar references to **at least one other part of the text**.

   In practice this means:

   Identification of commonality (eg theme, central relationship, importance of setting, use of imagery, development in characterisation, use of personal experience, use of dramatic devices or any other key element …)

   from the extract:

   1 relevant reference to technique; 1 appropriate comment

OR 1 relevant reference to idea; 1 appropriate comment

OR 1 relevant reference to feature; 1 appropriate comment

OR 1 relevant reference to text; 1 appropriate comment

(maximum of 2 marks only for discussion of extract)

from **at least one other part of the text**:

as above (x2) for **up to 4 marks**

PART A — DRAMA — *Sailmaker* **by Alan Spence**

6. Candidates should make four key points.

   Possible answers include:

   - Davie does not realise that Alec actually does need him/would like him to use his skills
   - Davie is already making excuses about not fixing up the yacht immediately
   - Davie indulges in unlawful gambling
   - Davie's lack of preparedness/homemaking skills
   - Does not provide financially for his family
   - asks Alec to go to the bookies for him against his will

7. For full marks candidates should identify two different aspects of Davie's mood, eg positive and negative, with supporting quotation/reference.

   Possible answers include:

   - **Lines 2–3:**

     Davie's mood is: sad, depressing, pessimistic, rejected, worthless, futile, angry etc (when discussing being made redundant as a sailmaker) "chucked"/"Nothin else doin"/"Nae work"/"Naebody needs sailmakers"

   - **Lines 10–16:**

     Davie's mood is optimistic, hopeful, humorous, excited, etc (when speaking about gambling) "wait an see"/"Who knows?"/"Maybe my coupon'll come up"/exaggerations about potential activity with winnings/"Never mind"/"Some ae these days"

8. (a) *Possible answers include:*

   - it is against the law to gamble
   - occasionally the bookmaker gets caught
   - gamblers protect their identity/avoid getting caught

   (b) Two clear points required for full marks (1 + 1).

   Possible answers include:

   - reveals he still considers himself a sailmaker pride/sense of identity/sense of importance

9. *Possible areas for comment include:*

   From the extract:

   - Alec gives Davie the yacht believing that he will fix it up represents his belief that Davie will live up to his promises.
   - Davie speaks knowledgably about the yacht revealing his past as a skilled worker.
   - Davie is already making excuses about why he can't fix up the yacht now.

   From elsewhere:

   - Alec speaks with admiration about his father's past as a Sailmaker to Ian, and believes that his dad will fix up the yacht for him to play with.

- Davie's continual lack of action in fixing the yacht represents his general procrastination in other matters/his bitterness at not being a Sailmaker/his prioritising (both in time and money) of gambling, drinking, etc.

- by contrast Billy paints the yacht immediately revealing that he is a different character who is proactive and keeps his word.

- Alec places the yacht in the Glory Hole when his dad loses his job as he realises this is not a good time for his dad to be reminded of it.

- Alec is accepting that his dad may not live up to his promises.

- in the final scene of the play the yacht is placed on the fire by Alec and Davie which shows an acceptance from Alec about the type of person/ father that Davie is.

- also represents the theme(s) of escape/childhood play, and relates to some of the music in the text, eg Red Sails in the Sunset, Will Your Anchor Hold, etc.

Candidates may choose to answer in **bullet points** in this final question, or write a number of linked statements. There is **no requirement** to write a "mini essay".

Up to 2 marks can be achieved for identifying elements of commonality as requested in the question. A further 2 marks can be achieved for **reference to the extract given.**

4 additional marks can be awarded for similar references to **at least one other part of the text.**

In practice this means:

Identification of commonality (eg theme, central relationship, importance of setting, use of imagery, development in characterisation, use of personal experience, use of dramatic devices or any other key element…)

from the extract:

1 relevant reference to technique; 1 appropriate comment

OR 1 relevant reference to idea; 1 appropriate comment

OR 1 relevant reference to feature; 1 appropriate comment

OR 1 relevant reference to text; 1 appropriate comment

(maximum of 2 marks only for discussion of extract)

from **at least one other part of the text:**

as above (x2) for **up to 4 marks**

PART A — DRAMA — Tally's Blood by Ann Marie Di Mambro

10. Candidates should make four key points for 1 mark each.

    Any four points.

    Possible answers include:

    - Bridget accuses Rosinella of making Lucia leave
    - Rosinella is confused about why Bridget is angry
    - Bridget accuses Rosinella of interfering in her relationship with Franco by making her feel that it wasn't genuine
    - Rosinella denies Bridget's accusations
    - Rosinella is annoyed that Bridget mentions Franco or their relationship
    - Rosinella expresses how upset she is that Lucia has left because of how much she loves her

    - Rosinella admits that she is glad that Lucia and Hughie will not be together
    - Rosinella wants to pretend this argument did not happen
    - Bridget reveals that she was pregnant with Franco's child

11. Candidates should deal with both word choice and sentence structure – 2 marks are available for each.

    1 mark for reference; 1 mark for comment (x2).

    Possible answers include:

    Word choice:

    - "you made me" eg suggests she is resentful of Rosinella's interference
    - "nothing (to him)" eg sense of worthlessness
    - "just a wee" eg sense of insignificance
    - "Scottish tart" eg lacking in importance or virtue
    - "no a day goes past…" eg lasting impact/ inescapable aspect
    - "Franco loved me" eg simplistic but bold statement

    Sentence structure:

    - use of/repetition of (Rosinella's) question eg to suggest her outrage
    - repeated "you" eg creating an accusatory tone
    - use of dash eg to suggest that Rosinella treated Bridget like an afterthought
    - short clipped sentence eg to show she powerfully disagrees with Rosinella
    - repetition of "Franco loved me." eg to suggest emphatic nature of her belief

12. Candidates should identify two different attitudes with a supporting reference for each attitude.

    1 mark for reference; 1 mark for comment (x2).

    Possible answers include:

    - confused eg use of questions/repeating Bridget's words
    - defensive eg "What did I ever do to you?"
    - annoyed eg "Angry"
    - rude eg calls Bridget "lady"
    - contemptuous eg "Dismissive"
    - trivialising eg "What you going on about now?"
    - shocked eg "shakes her head"/"backs off in disbelief"

13. *Possible areas for comment include:*

    From the extract:

    - family willing to defend each other eg Bridget taking on Rosinella for Hughie
    - family looking out for each other eg Rosinella and Massimo looking after Lucia even though she is not their child
    - family interfering in romantic relationships eg Rosinella disapproving of Hughie and Lucia as well as Bridget and Franco

From elsewhere:

- conflict eg family arguments about children not doing as expected by their parents or family (Massimo opening his own shop/Franco joining the army)
- love/loyalty: characters looking after family members eg Rosinella and her father in law, Bridget and Hughie with their mother and siblings, Rosinella and Massimo with Lucia

Candidates may choose to answer in **bullet points** in this final question, or write a number of linked statements. There is **no requirement** to write a "mini essay".

Up to 2 marks can be achieved for identifying elements of commonality as requested in the question. A further 2 marks can be achieved for **reference to the extract given.**

4 additional marks can be awarded for similar references to **at least one other part of the text.**

In practice this means:

Identification of commonality (eg theme, central relationship, importance of setting, use of imagery, development in characterisation, use of personal experience, use of dramatic devices or any other key element…)

from the extract:

1 relevant reference to technique; 1 appropriate comment

OR 1 relevant reference to idea; 1 appropriate comment

OR 1 relevant reference to feature; 1 appropriate comment

OR 1 relevant reference to text; 1 appropriate comment

(maximum of 2 marks only for discussion of extract)

from **at least one other part of the text:**

as above (x2) for **up to 4 marks**

PART B — PROSE — *The Cone-Gatherers* by Robin Jenkins

14. Candidates should explain how the writer uses two examples of language to effectively describe Roderick's imaginings.

    Reference should be made to lines 1–9.

    1 mark for reference; 1 mark for comment (x2).

    Possible answers include:

    Word choice:

    - "yew" has connotations of/links with death/Roderick imagines the cone-gatherers dead/murdered
    - "stalking" describes Duror's walk as predatory
    - "gloat" describes Duror's sense of smug satisfaction

    Contrast:

    - the reference to "tall"/"frowned" and "small"/"smiled" to illustrate the differences in the two men

    Sound:

    - (onomatopoeia of) "cracked" suggests the loud/clear/frightening sound of the gunfire

    Imagery:

    - "idea took root" links with trees and suggests the thought forming/developing in Roderick's mind
    - "green bony arms" personifies the branches and suggests care/support

Sentence structure:

- short sentence "That idea sprouted" adds impact due to its brevity. Suggests the importance of Roderick's thoughts

15. Candidates should explain two different ways in which Roderick thinks of death in lines 10–19.

    Candidates should use their own words as far as possible.

    Possible answers include:

    - "distant death was commonplace" — Roderick thinks of death as far away and/or a normal/regular occurrence
    - "loyally been pleased" — Roderick thinks it is honourable/death of enemy is a good thing/he is patriotic
    - "death … as a tyrant" — Roderick thought of death as cruel when it took someone he loved (his grandfather)/personally affected him
    - imagines the death of Duror as a sense of despair/damage/hopelessness…

16. Candidates should explain how the writer uses two examples of language to create a frightening atmosphere in lines 17–24.

    1 mark for reference; 1 mark for comment (x2).

    Possible answers include:

    - reference to "desolation" suggests world completely barren
    - reference to (every single leaf was) polluted suggests toxic atmosphere etc
    - image of deaths gathering to seek revenge suggests that Roderick fears his earlier loyalty/patriotism was wrong
    - question (about the death of evil and triumph of good) suggests that Roderick is unsure of the power of goodness
    - atmosphere of darkness and silence, created by lack of sun and birdsong suggests an eerie quiet/the calm before the storm
    - reference to the "hut in shadow" is typical of the horror genre/suggests evil to follow
    - Roderick is too frightened to either cry or pray suggests he is overcome by the power of evil in the wood

17. 1 mark for reference; 1 mark for comment (x2).

    Possible answers include:

    - "Without any interpretable gesture" suggests his actions are hard to understand/confusing
    - "without a sound" suggests stealth/sinister movements
    - "(turned and) vanished" suggests sudden/magical disappearance
    - "(as if this time) forever" suggests finality

18. Candidates should discuss why war is an important feature in this extract and elsewhere in the novel.

    Possible areas for comment include:

    - The setting of war is important as it places the characters in the wood at the same time: the brothers to gather cones, Duror to manage the estate and Lady Runcie-Campbell in charge in the absence of Sir Colin.

- **OR** the war reflects the conflict within and between a number of characters – eg within Duror/between him and the cone-gatherers/Roderick and the class system …

From the extract:

- Roderick is reminded of the war and its many deaths which he had initially greeted with patriotic loyalty
- **OR** the news of deaths heard on the radio is a regular feature and influences Roderick's thoughts of death in the woods, adding to his fears

From elsewhere:

- initial description of setting — idyllic with the subtle reference to the destroyer
- Duror is at war with himself — acknowledged on many occasions throughout the novel, often by references to sick/dying trees
- Duror's frustration at being too old to enlist partly fuels his hatred of the cone-gatherers
- Duror's wish to eliminate the cone-gatherers from the wood is linked to his sympathies for Hitler's actions against the Jews
- the war has allowed Duror to have the power that he has on the estate: Sir Colin is absent and Lady Runcie-Campbell relies on him for advice on estate management
- the wood is a microcosm of the world at war — Duror is waging his own war on the cone-gatherers whom he sees as inferior and should be eliminated; his own death at the end can be likened to Hitler's suicide

Candidates may choose to answer in **bullet points** in this final question, or write a number of linked statements. There is **no requirement** to write a "mini essay".

Up to 2 marks can be achieved for identifying elements of commonality as requested in the question. A further 2 marks can be achieved for **reference to the extract given.**

4 additional marks can be awarded for similar references to **at least one other part of the text.**

In practice this means:

Identification of commonality (eg theme, central relationship, importance of setting, use of imagery, development in characterisation, use of personal experience, use of dramatic devices or any other key element…)

from the extract:

1 relevant reference to technique; 1 appropriate comment

OR 1 relevant reference to idea; 1 appropriate comment

OR 1 relevant reference to feature; 1 appropriate comment

OR 1 relevant reference to text; 1 appropriate comment

(maximum of 2 marks only for discussion of extract)

from **at least one other part of the text:**

as above (x2) for **up to 4 marks**

PART B — PROSE — *The Testament of Gideon Mack* by James Robertson

19. Four relevant points for 1 mark each.

Candidates should use their own words as far as possible.

Possible answers include:

- Mack is discovered alive and with no serious injury his speedy recovery surprises doctors
- he doesn't seem keen to start back at his job
- he tells people about his ordeal and says he met the Devil who rescued him
- people think he has gone mad or similar and some are cross that he is saying things which are unchristian
- Mack takes the funeral of a friend but this is controversial as he speaks of meeting the Devil here too
- he is reported to the Presbytery
- there is a sort of a trial and Mack admits to what he has done but doesn't see anything wrong in it
- he is suspended until the main trial can take place but before that can happen Mack disappears

20. 1 mark for reference; 1 mark for comment (x2).

Possible answers include:

- "apparently" suggests it is not certain
- "(even more) amazingly" **OR** reference to parenthesis suggests incredulity
- "somehow" suggests near impossibility
- "no creature … survive" suggests he should not have lived through it
- "astonished" suggests no-one can believe it

21. 1 mark for reference; 1 mark for comment (x2).

Possible answers include:

- "no great hurry … duties" suggests lazy/distracted
- "claimed"/"improbable"/"unorthodox"/reference to the unlikely story suggests madness or delusions
- "assert"/"insisted" suggests he is convinced of it/ sure of himself/strength of character
- "frailty" suggests weakness
- "irreverent"/"scandalous"/"incompatible … minister"/"no option but to refer" suggests he is offensive/blasphemous

22. *Possible areas for comment include:*

- Candidates should identify one theme introduced in this extract and discuss how it is explored elsewhere in the novel.

Possible themes include:

- truth
- religion
- the supernatural
- stories within stories
- madness
- belief

Candidates may choose to answer in **bullet points** in this final question, or write a number of linked statements. There is **no requirement** to write a "mini essay".

Up to 2 marks can be achieved for identifying elements of commonality as requested in the question. A further 2 marks can be achieved for **reference to the extract given.**

4 additional marks can be awarded for similar references to **at least one other part of the text.**

In practice this means:

Identification of commonality (eg theme, central relationship, importance of setting, use of imagery, development in characterisation, use of personal experience, use of dramatic devices or any other key element...)

from the extract:

1 relevant reference to technique; 1 appropriate comment

OR 1 relevant reference to idea; 1 appropriate comment

OR 1 relevant reference to feature; 1 appropriate comment

OR 1 relevant reference to text; 1 appropriate comment

(maximum of 2 marks only for discussion of extract)

from **at least one other part of the text:**

as above (x2) for **up to 4 marks**

PART B — PROSE — *Kidnapped* by Robert Louis Stevenson

23. 1 mark for reference; 1 mark for comment (x2).

   Possible answers include:

   - "it was so dark inside"/"in the pitch darkness" suggests going into the unknown
   - "a body could scarce breathe" holding breath due to fear
   - "with a beating heart" infers heart beating fast due to danger
   - "Minding my uncle's word about the banisters" infers thinking about warning (outlined by his uncle)
   - "I pushed out with foot and hand" proceeded carefully due to fear
   - "by the touch" indicates caution as he feels his way in the dark
   - "felt my way" indicates caution as he feels his way in the dark

24. 1 mark for realisation; 1 mark for mood.

   Possible answers include:

   Realisation:
   - Ebenezer has tried to kill David by sending him to the tower

   Mood:
   - David feels furious/David wishes to gain some revenge for his uncle's actions/David is determined to get revenge even if it causes him harm in the process/David feels some bravery at the realisation

25. *Possible answers include:*
   - David reaches the top of the stairs
   - David realises there is nothing there
   - he discovers that the staircase ends suddenly
   - he realises he is in great danger/he could have died
   - he is physically affected by fear
   - he starts to make his way down
   - his downward journey is full of anger
   - the storm rises
   - he sees a light in the kitchen
   - he sees his uncle
   - there is loud thunder

26. 1 mark for reference; 1 mark for comment.

   Possible answers include:
   - "wind sprang up" emphasises the suddenness and speed that the wind appears
   - "clap" emphasises the physical power and suddenness of the wind
   - "died (again)" emphasises the speed that the wind disappeared
   - "it fell in buckets" the volume of rain is emphasised in that it seemed to be torrential
   - "blinding flash" the intensity of the lightning is emphasised
   - "tow-row" emphasises the very noisy nature of the thunder

27. *Possible areas for comment include:*
   - David's kidnapping
   - the roundhouse scene on the Covenant
   - the murder of Red Fox
   - the escape across the heather
   - the tension after the card game at Cluny's Cage
   - any of the many moments of tension between David and Alan throughout the novel
   - the confrontation with Ebenezer at the end of the novel

   Candidates may choose to answer in **bullet points** in this final question, or write a number of linked statements. There is **no requirement** to write a "mini essay".

   Up to 2 marks can be achieved for identifying elements of commonality as requested in the question. A further 2 marks can be achieved for **reference to the extract given**.

   4 additional marks can be awarded for similar references to **at least one other part of the text**.

   In practice this means:

   Identification of commonality (eg theme, central relationship, importance of setting, use of imagery, development in characterisation, use of personal experience, use of dramatic devices or any other key element...)

   from the extract:

   1 relevant reference to technique; 1 appropriate comment

   OR 1 relevant reference to idea; 1 appropriate comment

   OR 1 relevant reference to feature; 1 appropriate comment

   OR 1 relevant reference to text; 1 appropriate comment

   (maximum of 2 marks only for discussion of extract)

   from **at least one other part of the text:**

   as above (x2) for **up to 4 marks**

PART B — PROSE — *The Painter* by Iain Crichton Smith

28. 1 mark for reference; 1 mark for comment.

   Possible answers include:
   - "sitting comfortably"
     relaxed/at ease/calm
   - "no expression"
     impassive/detached/disengaged

- "cold clear intensity"/reference to alliteration indifferent/focused/unresponsive

29. 1 mark for reference; 1 mark for comment (x2).

Possible answers include:

- "scythes" is a dangerous implement
- "swing" highlights dangerous nature of weapons/how they were being used
- "contorted" suggests intensity/strength of their anger distorts their faces
- "fury" suggests fierce/angry nature of the encounter
- "(of) battle" suggests a fierce/powerful/hostile encounter
- "suffused" suggests full of/consumed/visibly roused
- "blood" suggests violence/harm
- "(and) rage" suggests intense/deep-rooted/passionate hatred for each other
- Repetition of "as" conveys the energy/tension/physical nature of the fight
- "teeth drawn ... snarl" suggests animal-like brutality

30. *Possible answers include:*

"admiration"

- his ability to remain focused on his work
- the depth/single-mindedness of his focus
- his disregard for his own safety

"bitter disgust"

- his detachment/isolation from the villagers ("gaze ... beyond the human")
- his impartial/unemotional stance
- his coldness/superiority to those around him (comparison to hawk)
- his reaction to the disruption to his painting ("blind fury")
- his visible emotion relating to the conflict ("tears of rage"/"still snarling")
- his departure from the conflict with the narrator

31. *Possible answers include:*

- he is ignored
- they are troubled by him/they don't understand him
- he is seen as being different/an outsider
- he is rejected
- his work is destroyed
- he does not conform with their code of conduct

32. *Possible areas for comment include:*

- **"The Telegram"** — the "thin woman's" reputation as an outsider due to the sacrifices she has made for her son
- **"The Red Door"** — Murdo's discontent leading to his desire to be independent from the constraints of village life; Mary's independence shown by her choice of clothing/creativity etc.
- **"Mother and Son"** — John's isolation from his peers/lack of confidence due to his mother's constant criticism/control/dominance

- **"In Church"** — "The priest" (a deserter who is in hiding) is at odds with society, having lost all sense of humanity
- **"The Crater"** — Robert feels at odds with his role as an Officer in a war time situation

Candidates may choose to answer in **bullet points** in this final question, or write a number of linked statements. There is **no requirement** to write a "mini essay".

Up to 2 marks can be achieved for identifying elements of commonality as requested in the question. A further 2 marks can be achieved for **reference to the extract given.**

4 additional marks can be awarded for similar references to **at least one other part of the text.**

In practice this means:

Identification of commonality (eg theme, central relationship, importance of setting, use of imagery, development in characterisation, use of personal experience, use of dramatic devices or any other key element...)

from the extract:

1 relevant reference to technique; 1 appropriate comment

OR 1 relevant reference to idea; 1 appropriate comment

OR 1 relevant reference to feature; 1 appropriate comment

OR 1 relevant reference to text; 1 appropriate comment

(maximum of 2 marks only for discussion of extract)

from **at least one other part of the text:**

as above (x2) for **up to 4 marks**

PART B — PROSE — *Dear Santa* by Anne Donovan

33. Four points for 1 mark each.

Possible answers include:

- Alison is writing a letter to Santa
- she is trying to ask him to make her mother love her
- she is finding writing the letter difficult
- she doesn't believe Santa can make her mother love her
- she isn't sure if she believes in Santa
- she is feeling unhappy/pessimistic
- her mother comes into the bedroom/looks after Katie/spends time with Alison
- Alison finishes the letter but does not ask for what she really wants
- Alison and her mother spend some close/loving time together
- Alison demonstrates her affection for her mother
- Alison's mother demonstrates a little affection towards Alison
- at the end of the extract it is suggested there is hope for their relationship

34. 1 mark for reference; 1 mark for comment.

Possible answers include:

- "the page ah'm starin at" suggests it is hard for her to start the letter
- "it's hard tae find the words" shows she finds it difficult to say what she really wants/feels

- unfinished sentences emphasise how hard she finds it to put her feelings into words
- repeated questions suggest she doubts her request would work
- negative answers reinforce the fact that she doubts whether a letter to Santa would be effective
- reference to grey outside/no white Christmas reflects the negativity of her mood
- the fact that she doesn't write down what she actually wants shows she doesn't think it's achievable

35. (a) 1 mark for reference; 1 mark for comment.

Possible answers include:

- "Hair glowin like a halo" — suggests angelic, connotations of goodness, bringing light into darkness, positivity, etc
- (hair) "soft and fuzzy" — makes the mother seem kind and gentle
- "she's in a good mood" etc, suggests she's mellowed towards Alison and is allowing her to be closer
- "There's nothing wrang wi broon hair" suggests she understands Alison wants to be more like her and Katie but she reassures her that she is fine the way she is
- "She looks at me mair soft like" — suggests more loving
- "She kisses me" — suggests affection
- "nearly", or reference to "a wee crack of light" suggests hope that the relationship can be rebuilt/ that there is some love there

(b) 1 mark for reference; 1 mark for comment.

Possible answers showing negative contrast include:

- "she cannae be bothered wi that"/"jerks her heid away"/"sayin don't"/"you'll mess it up" suggests mother doesn't like physical contact with Alison
- "dry (kiss)" suggests limited, grudging, etc
- "barely grazing" suggests mother hasn't much time for Alison
- "before ah've kissed her back" suggests she does not really want physical contact with Alison
- "closin the door" suggests putting up a barrier between herself and Alison, or similar

36. *Possible areas for comment include:*

- **"Virtual Pals"** — Siobhan's lack of confidence; boyfriend issues; growing up; relationships
- **"Zimmerobics"** — old age and associated problems; loneliness
- **"All that Glisters"** — how Clare copes with her father's illness and death; how she copes with difficult adults such as the shopkeeper and her aunt; how she overcomes challenges; how she supports her mother in her grief; how she celebrates her daddy
- **"A Chitterin Bite"** — relationships; lack of confidence; inability to move on; as a child, Mary does not deal well with Agnes growing up and moving on; as an adult, she resolves her personal difficulties by taking control and ending the affair

Candidates may choose to answer in **bullet points** in this final question, or write a number of linked statements. There is **no requirement** to write a "mini essay".

Up to 2 marks can be achieved for identifying elements of commonality as requested in the question. A further 2 marks can be achieved for **reference to the extract given**.

4 additional marks can be awarded for similar references to **at least one other part of the text**.

<u>In practice this means:</u>

Identification of commonality (eg theme, central relationship, importance of setting, use of imagery, development in characterisation, use of personal experience, use of dramatic devices or any other key element...)

from the extract:

1 relevant reference to technique; 1 appropriate comment

OR 1 relevant reference to idea; 1 appropriate comment

OR 1 relevant reference to feature; 1 appropriate comment

OR 1 relevant reference to text; 1 appropriate comment

(maximum of 2 marks only for discussion of extract)

from **at least one other part of the text**:

as above (x2) for **up to 4 marks**

PART C — POETRY — *Originally* by Carol Ann Duffy

37. 1 mark for each point made. Candidates must use their own words.

Possible answers include:

- gloss of "red room" — reference to vehicle
- gloss of "fell" — travelled downhill/in a downwards direction
- gloss of "through the fields" — travelled through the country/countryside
- gloss of "mother singing" — reference to her mother's voice
- gloss of "My brothers cried"/"bawling" — brothers being upset
- gloss of "miles rushed back ... etc" — sense of leaving somewhere/distance
- gloss of "toy ... holding its paw, etc" — had comfort of toy/teddy

38. 1 mark for reference; 1 mark for comment (x2).

Possible answers include:

- "slow" a gradual awareness of the new surroundings/a gradual build-up of feelings in response to the move
- "leaving you standing" you find yourself isolated
- "resigned" you have to accept things/learn to accept things
- "up an avenue" you can be lonely
- "sudden" change can seem quick/unexpected
- "Your accent wrong" you feel out of place/don't fit in
- "unimagined" you haven't been able to picture new surroundings

- "pebble-dashed estates" find yourself in unfamiliar surroundings
- "big boys eating worms" people seem very different
- "shouting words you don't understand" language barriers
- "parents' anxiety" you sense other people's worries
- "stirred like a loose tooth" you become aware that things are different
- "I want our own country" you miss your old surroundings/want to return

39. 1 mark for reference; 1 mark for comment (x2).

    Possible answers include:

    - "But" suggests a change from being an outsider to accepting her new surroundings
    - "then you forget/don't recall" suggests your memory blots out old life
    - "change" you adapt to your surroundings
    - "brother swallow a slug" suggests awareness that other family members are accepting the local culture
    - "skelf of shame" suggests how little guilt is felt in accepting the local culture
    - "my tongue … snake" suggests a casting off of old life, just as a snake casts off its old skin
    - "my voice … like the rest" suggests she's fitting in with the local culture

40. 1 mark for reference; 1 mark for comment.

    Possible answers include:

    - the use of the title "Originally" rounds off/brings a sense of closure
    - the use of "Originally" links back to the discussion of where you come from/your origins (an important theme of the poem)
    - "hesitates" suggests uncertainty about national/cultural identity (one of the main themes of the poem)/suggests acceptance of new surroundings

41. *Possible areas for comment include:*

    - **"Originally"** – memory, identity/sense of belonging/acceptance/isolation, etc
    - **"War Photographer"** – memory, painful memories, human cruelty, etc
    - **"Valentine"** – different aspects of love, relationships, etc
    - **"Havisham"** – jealousy/hard heartedness, rejection, etc
    - **"Anne Hathaway"** – love, relationships, etc
    - **"Mrs Midas"** – love, relationships, change, etc

    Other answers are possible.

    Candidates may choose to answer in **bullet points** in this final question, or write a number of linked statements. There is **no requirement** to write a "mini essay".

    Up to 2 marks can be achieved for identifying elements of commonality as requested in the question. A further 2 marks can be achieved for **reference to the extract given.**

    4 additional marks can be awarded for similar references to **at least one other part of the text.**

In practice this means:

Identification of commonality (eg theme, central relationship, importance of setting, use of imagery, development in characterisation, use of personal experience, use of dramatic devices or any other key element…)

from the extract:

1 relevant reference to technique; 1 appropriate comment

OR 1 relevant reference to idea; 1 appropriate comment

OR 1 relevant reference to feature; 1 appropriate comment

OR 1 relevant reference to text; 1 appropriate comment

(maximum of 2 marks only for discussion of extract)

from **at least one other part of the text:**

as above (x2) for **up to 4 marks**

PART C — POETRY — *Good Friday* by Edwin Morgan

42. Two references plus comments on what we learn about the drunken man.

    1 mark for reference; 1 mark for comment (x2).

    Possible answers include:

    - "D's this go"/"right along Bath Street?" shows that he's confused
    - "I've got to get some Easter eggs for the kiddies" shows he is kind/generous
    - "I don't say it's right" **OR** "I'm no saying it's right" shows he is aware that his drinking on a religious holiday could be disagreed with
    - "ye understand — ye understand?" shows that he wants the poet to empathise/doesn't want to be judged harshly
    - "I'm no boring you, eh?" shows his desire to be listened to/accepted

43. (a) 1 mark for reference; 1 mark for comment.

    Possible answers include:

    - use of Glaswegian dialect suggests sense of place
    - use of second person suggests the man is speaking directly to someone else
    - use of long winding sentences suggests the man is rambling
    - use of dashes/pauses suggests hesitation/loss of train of thought
    - use of questions suggests he's seeking agreement
    - use of repetition suggests immediacy of speech

    (b) 1 mark for reference; 1 mark for identification of idea or concern (x2).

    Possible answers include:

    - "take today, I don't know what today's in aid of" suggests eg (religious) ignorance
    - "whether Christ was — crucified or was he–" suggests eg religious doubt/ignorance
    - "You're an educatit man, you can tell me" suggests eg awareness of class/educational differences
    - "the working man has nae education" suggests eg awareness of lack of opportunities
    - "he's just bliddy ignorant" suggests eg awareness/acceptance of lack of education

44. For 2 marks, candidates should refer to a feature of the last five lines and how it effectively continues an idea/language feature from earlier in the poem.

Possible answers include:

- "The bus brakes violently" echoes the opening lines which focus on the bus's movements
- "He lunges for the stair, swings down – off" echoes the opening lines which focus on the drunken man's movements
- "for his Easter eggs" recalls the drunk man's task/setting in time/title
- the structure of the last few lines

  OR

  > "on very
  >
  >   nearly
  >
  >   steady
  >
  >   legs"

  emphasises the man's drunkenness

45. *Possible comments on other poems:*

- **"Good Friday"** – religion, compassion, class in terms of education
- **"Trio"** – supernatural, passing of time, alienation, religion
- **"Slate"** – change, ie making a fresh start (politically or personally), change over time, adapting to change, identity, hopeful
- **"Hyena"** – death, brutality, survival, isolation, fear, perseverance of the hunter, alienation through fear, suffering
- **"In the Snack Bar"** – determination, compassion, isolation, perseverance, alienation, helplessness, suffering
- **"Winter"** – death and the relentless passing of time, progress of time, aging, suffering

Candidates may choose to answer in **bullet points** in this final question, or write a number of linked statements. There is **no requirement** to write a "mini essay".

Up to 2 marks can be achieved for identifying elements of commonality as requested in the question. A further 2 marks can be achieved for **reference to the extract given**.

4 additional marks can be awarded for similar references to **at least one other part of the text**.

In practice this means:

Identification of commonality (eg theme, central relationship, importance of setting, use of imagery, development in characterisation, use of personal experience, use of dramatic devices or any other key element...)

from the extract:

1 relevant reference to technique; 1 appropriate comment

OR 1 relevant reference to idea; 1 appropriate comment

OR 1 relevant reference to feature; 1 appropriate comment

OR 1 relevant reference to text; 1 appropriate comment

(**maximum of 2 marks only for discussion of extract**)

from **at least one other part of the text**:

as above (x2) for **up to 4 marks**

PART C — POETRY — *Sounds of the Day* by Norman MacCaig

46. Two points for 2 marks.

Possible answers include:

- he seems unconcerned/untroubled by them
- he seems comforted by them
- he reacts to them in a positive way
- they are familiar to him

47. 1 mark for reference; 1 mark for comment.

Possible answers include:

- "clatter" is a harsh/unsettling sound
- "creak" is an eerie sound/suggestive of the "door scraped shut" (which is to follow in line 10)
- "snuffling" suggests crying
- "puff" suggests something sudden
- "seeing us off" suggests aggression/parting
- "blocking ... unblocking" lack of constancy/ever changing
- "black drums rolled" suggests portent/sign of trouble
- "falling" suggests doom/troubling consequences

48. 1 mark for reference; 1 mark for comment (x2).

Possible answers include:

- "(door) scraped (shut)" harsh sound/contrasting sound with earlier (relative) calm
- "shut" is final/ominous
- "(the) end" suggests closed off/cut off/finality
- "all the sounds" suggests an all-encompassing change
- "you (left me)" contrast with "us" from verse 1/sense of separation
- "left me" suggests isolation/loneliness/upset
- "quietest fire" suggests silence/is opposite of earlier normal sounds/oxymoron/paradox/superlative

49. 1 mark for reference; 1 mark for comment (x2).

Possible answers include:

- "I thought" suggests poet's uncertainty
- "hurt in my pride only" suggests initial limited impact
- "forgetting that" suggests impact was not immediate
- "plunge" impact was deep
- "freezing (water)" suggests cold/unpleasant effects
- "ice" suggests extreme coldness of feeling
- identification of image of "bangle of ice" image suggests memories/burden of memory/weight of memory
- "whole" suggests completeness of effect
- "numb" suggests he has been overwhelmed, etc

50. *Possible areas for comment include:*

- **"Assisi"** – feelings of anger, outrage, bitterness
- **"Aunt Julia"** – feelings of nostalgia, loss, confusion, etc
- **"Basking Shark"** – feelings of confusion, doubt, shock, etc
- **"Visiting Hour"** – feelings of sadness, loss, unworthiness, etc
- **"Memorial"** – sadness, loss, etc

Candidates may choose to answer in **bullet points** in this final question, or write a number of linked statements. There is **no requirement** to write a "mini essay".

Up to 2 marks can be achieved for identifying elements of commonality as requested in the question. A further 2 marks can be achieved for **reference to the extract given**.

4 additional marks can be awarded for similar references to **at least one other part of the text**.

In practice this means:

Identification of commonality (eg theme, central relationship, importance of setting, use of imagery, development in characterisation, use of personal experience, use of dramatic devices or any other key element...)

from the extract:

1 relevant reference to technique; 1 appropriate comment

OR 1 relevant reference to idea; 1 appropriate comment

OR 1 relevant reference to feature; 1 appropriate comment

OR 1 relevant reference to text; 1 appropriate comment

(maximum of 2 marks only for discussion of extract)

from **at least one other part of the text:**

as above (x2) for **up to 4 marks**

PART C — POETRY — *Keeping Orchids* **by Jackie Kay**

51. Candidates must use their own words as far as possible.

1 mark for a valid answer (x2).

Possible answers include:

- the (first person) narrator describes what happens when she meets her mother for the first time
- there is an awkward atmosphere between the two women
- the mother gives the narrator flowers (orchids)
- orchids are rare/exotic and (therefore) difficult to look after/this symbolises the precarious nature of their relationship
- the vase of flowers spills twice /symbolises the fragile nature of their relationship
- the narrator tries to sort out the flower arrangement but she is not good at it/symbolises her feelings of awkwardness
- some of the buds stay shut
- the narrator sees the flowers as a burden/ responsibility (not a pleasure)

52. Word choice: 1 mark for reference; 1 mark for comment.

Structure: 1 mark for reference; 1 mark for comment.

Possible answers of word choice include:

- "first (met)" establishes the importance of that moment
- "twelve days later" shows how much time has elapsed since the meeting
- "Twice since" shows the effort put in to take the flowers home
- "Even after that" shows that time seems to be against the flowers

- repetition of "twelve days later" reiterates the distance since the meeting time
- "fading fast" suggests the haziness of time passing

Possible answers on structure include:

- the poem is written in couplets which gives a regular (predictable) pace/rhythm to indicate time passing steadily
- there is repeated use of enjambment to indicate the pace of events
- the frequent use of conjunctives moves the story of the poem forward at a fast pace
- parenthesis is limited indicating the urgency to recount only the basic account of what happened
- short sentences indicate the poet's intention to summarise events as succinctly as possible
- repetition of "twice since" reiterates frequency of an event

53. 1 mark for reference; 1 mark for comment (x3).

Possible answers include:

- "voice rushes through a tunnel the other way" suggests distance
- "try to remember" shows lack of clarity/shows the physical distance
- "a paisley pattern scarf, a brooch" suggests the mother is dressed up for the occasion
- "her hands, awkward and hard to hold" suggests lack of familiarity of touch
- "fold and unfold" suggests the mother is fidgeting
- "the story of her life" suggests lack of familiarity
- "Compressed" suggests stiffness/only revealing the bare minimum of details
- "Airtight" suggests defensiveness/being impenetrable

54. *Possible areas for comment include:*

- the difference between appearance and reality
- the conflict within family relationships
- the difficulties of parenthood
- the changing roles we perform as family members
- the influence of time in shaping our memories/point of view
- the importance of setting in shaping our behaviour/ influencing our thinking
- the complex nature of love
- the acceptance of imperfection
- the development of self-awareness through time
- the complexities of degeneration/decay

Candidates may choose to answer in **bullet points** in this final question, or write a number of linked statements. There is **no requirement** to write a "mini essay".

Up to 2 marks can be achieved for identifying elements of commonality as requested in the question. A further 2 marks can be achieved for **reference to the extract given**.

4 additional marks can be awarded for similar references to **at least one other part of the text**.

<u>In practice this means:</u>

Identification of commonality (eg theme, central relationship, importance of setting, use of imagery, development in characterisation, use of personal experience, use of dramatic devices or any other key element...)

from the extract:

1 relevant reference to technique; 1 appropriate comment

OR 1 relevant reference to idea; 1 appropriate comment

OR 1 relevant reference to feature; 1 appropriate comment

OR 1 relevant reference to text; 1 appropriate comment

(maximum of 2 marks only for discussion of extract)

from **at least one other part of the text:**

as above (x2) for **up to 4 marks**

SECTION 2 – CRITICAL ESSAY

Please see the assessment criteria for the Critical Essay on page 131.

Acknowledgements

Permission has been sought from all relevant copyright holders and Hodder Gibson is grateful for the use of the following:

An extract adapted from the article 'Me, Boris Johnson and our brilliantly hands-off parents' by Rachel Johnson © The Times/News Syndication, 15 October 2012 (2014 Reading for Understanding, Analysis and Evaluation pages 2 & 3);
An extract from 'Bold Girls' copyright © 1991 Rona Munro. Excerpted with permission of Nick Hern Books Ltd: www.nickhernbooks.co.uk (2014 Critical Reading page 2);
An extract from 'Sailmaker' by Alan Spence. Reproduced by permission of Hodder Education (2014 Critical Reading page 4);
An extract from 'Tally's Blood' by Ann Marie di Mambro, published by Education Scotland. Reprinted by permission of Ann Marie di Mambro/MacFarlane Chard Associates (2014 Critical Reading pages 6 & 7);
An extract from 'The Cone-Gatherers' by Robin Jenkins, published by Canongate Books Ltd. (2014 Critical Reading page 8);
An extract from 'The Testament Of Gideon Mack' by James Robertson (Hamish Hamilton 2006, Penguin Books 2007). Copyright © James Robertson, 2006. Reproduced by permission of Penguin Books Ltd. (2014 Critical Reading pages 10 & 11);
An extract from 'Kidnapped' by Robert Louis Stevenson, published by Cassell and Company Ltd 1886. Public domain (2014 Critical Reading pages 12 & 13);
An extract from 'Telegram' by Iain Crichton Smith, taken from 'The Red Door: The Complete English Stories 1949–76', published by Birlinn. Reproduced by permission of Birlinn Ltd. www.birlinn.co.uk (2014 Critical Reading page 14);
An extract from 'Away In A Manger' by Anne Donovan, taken from 'Hieroglyphics and Other Stories', published by Canongate Books Ltd. (2014 Critical Reading page 16);
The poem, 'War Photographer' by Carol Ann Duffy, taken from 'New Selected Poems 1984–2004' (Picador, 2004). Reproduced by permission of the author c/o Rogers, Coleridge & White Ltd., 20 Powis Mews, London W11 1JN (2014 Critical Reading page 18);
The poem 'In the Snack-bar' by Edwin Morgan, taken from 'New Selected Poems', published by Carcanet Press Limited 2000 (2014 Critical Reading pages 20 & 21);
The poem, 'Basking Shark' by Norman MacCaig, taken from 'The Poems of Norman MacCaig' edited by Ewan McCaig, published by Polygon. Reproduced by permission of Birlinn Ltd. www.birlinn.co.uk (2014 Critical Reading page 22);
The poem 'Lucozade' by Jackie Kay, taken from 'Darling: New & Selected Poems' (Bloodaxe Books, 2007). Reprinted with permission of Bloodaxe Books, on behalf of the author. www.bloodaxebooks.com (2014 Critical Reading page 24);
An extract adapted from the article 'Missing penalty not end of world but a chance to learn more about life' by Matthew Syed © The Times/News Syndication, 9th July 2014 (2015 Reading for Understanding, Analysis and Evaluation pages 2 & 3);
An extract from 'Bold Girls' copyright © 1991 Rona Munro. Excerpted with permission of Nick Hern Books Ltd: www.nickhernbooks.co.uk (2015 Critical Reading pages 2 & 3);
An extract from 'Sailmaker' by Alan Spence. Reproduced by permission of Hodder Education (2015 Critical Reading page 4);
An extract from 'Tally's Blood' by Ann Marie di Mambro, published by Education Scotland. Reprinted by permission of Ann Marie di Mambro/MacFarlane Chard Associates (2015 Critical Reading pages 6 & 7);
An extract from 'The Cone-Gatherers' by Robin Jenkins, published by Canongate Books Ltd. (2015 Critical Reading page 8);
An extract from 'The Testament Of Gideon Mack' by James Robertson (Hamish Hamilton 2006, Penguin Books 2007). Copyright © James Robertson, 2006. Reproduced by permission of Penguin Books Ltd. (2015 Critical Reading pages 10 & 11);
An extract from 'Kidnapped' by Robert Louis Stevenson, published by Cassell and Company Ltd 1886. Public domain (2015 Critical Reading pages 12 & 13);
An extract from 'Mother and Son' by Iain Crichton Smith, taken from 'The Red Door: The Complete English Stories 1949–76', published by Birlinn. Reproduced by permission of Birlinn Ltd. www.birlinn.co.uk (2015 Critical Reading page 14);
An extract from 'All that Glisters' by Anne Donovan, taken from 'Hieroglyphics and Other Stories', published by Canongate Books Ltd. (2015 Critical Reading page 16);
The poem, 'Valentine' by Carol Ann Duffy, taken from 'New Selected Poems 1984–2004' (Picador, 2004). Reproduced by permission of the author c/o Rogers, Coleridge & White Ltd., 20 Powis Mews, London W11 1JN (2015 Critical Reading page 18);
The poem 'Hyena' by Edwin Morgan, taken from 'From Glasgow to Saturn', published by Carcanet Press Limited 1973 (2015 Critical Reading pages 20 & 21);
The poem 'Visiting Hour' by Norman MacCaig, taken from 'The Poems of Norman MacCaig' edited by Ewan McCaig, published by Polygon. Reproduced by permission of Birlinn Ltd. www.birlinn.co.uk (2015 Critical Reading page 22);